DE-FRAGMENTING
MODERNITY

DE-FRAGMENTING
MODERNITY

Reintegrating
Knowledge with Wisdom,
Belief with Truth,
and Reality with Being

Paul Tyson

CASCADE *Books* • Eugene, Oregon

Cascade Books
An Imprint of Wipf and Stock Publishers
199 W. 8th Ave., Suite 3
Eugene, OR 97401

www.wipfandstock.com

PAPERBACK ISBN: 978-1-5326-1464-4
HARDCOVER ISBN: 978-1-5326-1466-8
EBOOK ISBN: 978-1-5326-1465-1

Cataloguing-in-Publication data:

Names: Tyson, Paul G.

Title: De-fragmenting modernity : reintegrating knowledge with wisdom, belief with truth, and reality with being / Paul Tyson.

Description: Eugene, OR: Cascade Books, 2017 | Includes bibliographical references.

Identifiers: ISBN 978-1-5326-1464-4 (paperback) | ISBN 978-1-5326-1466-8 (hardcover) | ISBN 978-1-5326-1465-1 (ebook)

Subjects: LCSH: Civilization, Modern | Philosophical Theology | Faith | Knowledge, Theory of | Metaphysics | Ontology

Classification: BR115.G54 T97 2017 (paperback) | BR115.G54 (ebook)

Manufactured in the U.S.A.   06/07/17

CONTENTS

1

SOLVABLE AND UN-SOLVABLE PROBLEMS

Un-solvable Problems

Maurice Blondel has said that there are no more difficult problems to solve than those that do not exist.[1] What he means is that if we do not understand what our real problems are our most intelligent problem solving strategies will fail to make any impact on reality. Genuine solutions to real problems do not follow from a miss-assigned understanding of what the real problem is.

Alas, misidentifying problems and the resultant flurry of ineffective action are a stubborn feature of modern technocratic power. In Australia—where I live—our well-meaning government provides us with many illustrations of Blondel's truism. Let us take just one example.

For the past twenty years my federal government has been trying to reduce our alarming youth suicide statistics. By every statistical measure our government's efforts have failed. We have raised public awareness of the problem, sought to de-stigmatize self-harming behavior, we have taught our health workers and counsellors the most up-to-date techniques in the

1. Blondel, *Action*, 16.

1

psychological treatment and pastoral care of self-harming youth, but all to no avail. The rate of youth suicide continues to rise.

A key aspect of this tragic failure is the technocratic grid through which "the problem" and its likely "solutions" are seen. This grid has to make "the problem" of a statistical increase in youth suicide amenable to the categories of implementable policies that can be rolled out in nation-wide prevention programs. All this is done within the functionally materialist parameters of secular knowledge; a way of "seeing" both the problem and the solutions that is blind to existential and spiritual drivers. Treating youth suicide as if it is an essentially psychological problem (that is, treating psychological problems as if they have no existential and spiritual dynamics) is to try to treat symptoms rather than address causes if the problem actually has existential and spiritual drivers. Of course, psychological therapy may well be helpful to deeply traumatized young people. Perhaps the increase in youth suicide would have been considerably worse had our government not tried to provide psychologically framed public health measures to counter youth suicide. But various forms of self-harm among our youth are now so widespread, and the fact that an increasing proportion of young people who are "at risk" are from "normal" families indicates that factors other than clinical psychological trauma are at play in the overall trend.

Could it be that we are misidentifying despair and anomia as depression?

This is a question our policy controllers cannot ask because psychologically defined public health challenges are problems our technocrats think they can solve, but despair and anomia are not. At a policy level, we are more or less locked into seeking "mental health" answers to the youth suicide problem, so we put psychologists at the front line of strategic planning to reverse the problem. But to do so is to define the limits of what "the problem" can and cannot be, regardless of whether those limits actually define our real problem.

Our psychological profession, at least in Australia, is embedded in behaviorist reductionism, located decisively within what Charles Taylor calls an immanent frame.[2] This outlook sees existential and spiritual concerns as epiphenomenal constructs that are secondary to the *real* drivers of human behavior. So our experts and policy boffins systematically treat depressive symptoms as if they are the primal causes of the problem. Further, if youth suicide is at least in part symptomatic of a cultural and community malaise,

---

2. Taylor, *A Secular Age*, 539–93.

again, treating self-harming individuals is not going to address the real problem. And it is not hard to see that a culture that promotes narcissism, relational atomization, and the absence of any substantive conception of transcendent meaning in daily life is now strongly embedded in the norms of our consumer lifestyle. If we define psychological "health" as simply what is functionally normative to any given shared way of life—what sociologists call a life-form—there is something inherently misguided about pathologizing a "natural" feature of that life-form without asking if the life-form itself is pathological.

Since Durkheim, sociologists have known that one of the characteristic features of structuring society around high levels of negative freedom is a certain background level of despair and anomia. That is, when modern liberal societies are set up so that individuals can please themselves and choose their own values and beliefs as much as possible (negative freedom—freedom *from* external restraint), collective customs of appropriate behavior and common religious and ethical belief structures are seriously diluted. At a certain level of dilution, this dynamic dissolves the shared customary framework of a common way of living governed by shared beliefs about cosmic order. This renders power structures bleakly functional and impersonal, meaning subjective and insubstantial, and behavior norms—manners, common customs of propriety—highly plastic and uncertain. This produces anomia and despair: confusion about cosmic order expressed as a debilitating existential anxiety about one's own and other people's intentions, identity, and significance. So if the norm of mental health we are aiming at is not prepared to put individualistic consumerism itself on the table as the possible problem, then—in Blondel's sense—our policy makers may well be trying to solve the problem of youth suicide without seeing the problem as it really is. This may account for why our best efforts at solving this problem have failed so decisively. For problems that do not exist are impossible to solve.

It seems to me that there are some basic features of the reality in which we live that have become invisible and even incomprehensible to our technocratic conception of valid knowledge and effective action. We have, I suspect, developed a way of life that is entrenched in a set of cultural blind spots that are unwittingly causing us serious problem solving grief. Let us look quickly at a few further examples that concretely spell out what type of blind spots we have.

Four Scenarios

We know how to isolate the inner cell mass of very early human embryos in order to harvest their stem cells. We know that embryonic stem cells can be differentiated into any cell type and they have amazing powers of propagation. We know the clinical possibilities for tissue replacement in diseased or damaged patients is greatly enhanced by these findings and techniques. These are the facts. But what is the human *meaning*, what are the moral *implications*, and what is the transcendently referenced *significance* of "harvesting" human embryos as a medical technology? These are not questions that an informed knowledge of the scientific facts and technological possibilities can answer.

We know that currency and derivative trading is now denominated in monetary flows that are orders of magnitude greater than the real global economy in the production and distribution of actual goods and services. We know that there is a global system of financial secrecy jurisdictions used by transnational corporations and the super-rich to bypass nationally located tax responsibilities. We know that wherever possible, governments will bail out "too big to fail" private financial institutions if they get into serious trouble. So we know that the wealth of the world is being continuously siphoned upward toward a tiny transnational super-elite and the elected leaders of nations are increasingly irrelevant (other than as guarantors) to real financial and economic power. But this is the "reality" of how the global financial system works, so we work with it. Whether it is right or wrong, fair or exploitative, democratic or tyrannical is more or less irrelevant to its "reality." We accept the amorality of high financial power.

We accept the amorality of high geopolitical power too. Who is going to argue right and wrong with the global military power of the USA? Our "realist" view of power maintains that actors always pursue their own interests, and this means that the most powerful have the most power to get what suits them. Practically, "in the real world," questions of right and wrong—as if might and right are different sorts of things—simply don't apply to great power.

In theory, most of us probably support universal human rights. Including the rights of refugees to seek asylum and permanent re-settlement in UNHCR Refugee Convention signatory countries. In practice, many Europeans, Americans, and Australians are scared of Islamic asylum seekers. We are scared of their religion, we are scared that they are terrorist, we are scared that they will take our jobs and drain the wealth of our nation when we ourselves already feel insecure and vulnerable. So, in practice, the principle of universal human rights is not sacred to us. We water it down if our politicians feel they can make electoral mileage out of refusing asylum seekers refuge. We Westerners like to think of ourselves as tolerant pluralists, but we often do not understand the way non-Christian people do religion, and it scares us. We like to think of ourselves as good people, but when we feel insecure and vulnerable, we feel entitled to drop universal and costly moral responsibilities. Are not morals just made up anyway? Aren't they just socially constructed conventions? Why shouldn't we tweak them to suit ourselves when we need to?

We know what facts are. But can we *know* what things mean, can we *know* what the value of things is, can we *know* if any spiritual reality stands over our realm of practical action and judges it? Our knowledge doesn't give us answers to these questions. Why doesn't our knowledge help us here?

The Problem

Modern Western knowledge is blind to truths of being and belief. This is a unique signature of our culture, and by and large, we are proud of it. To us, only facts are true, the very idea of "being" hardly makes sense, and anything to do with "belief" sits in the realm of personal conviction.

Our freedom to believe whatever we want about meaning and value means that truth simply doesn't apply to belief. Facts are true and not false, as adjudicated by science, but radically incompatible belief options all reside together like a menagerie of gods in a well-ordered pantheon. Regarding beliefs, individuals choose their own gods and our tolerant society rejoices in personal conviction pluralism (within limits). This is workable because personal beliefs are subservient to public facts and legal behaviors. Factual things and legal regulations unite us—these are our master gods—but we are free to go our own way in religion, value commitments, and (I know this word doesn't mean a lot today) being.

Despite Western culture's deep embedding in classical Greek thinking, our civilization now has almost no conception of truth in relation to being. To the ancient Greeks, the investigation of "being" is a truth-seeking enterprise that concerns itself with essential, non-material reality. While defining essential truths in terms of "being" is a distinctly Greek move, the idea that spiritual reality concerns the most primary level of the real is, apart from us moderns, a civilizational and cultural mainstay of the human condition. Our separation of truth from being, and from believing, makes us different from every other civilization.

Interestingly, the Western discourse of Progress is deeply aware of the civilizational uniqueness of Western modernity. Correctly, we link this difference to modern scientific knowledge. Because we have science, and because secular scientific rationality so deeply orders our way of life, we see ourselves as having *advanced* beyond our pre-modern origins. We think of the Middle Ages as *pre*-modern, not merely in temporal terms, but in terms of its lack of progressive development. The Middle Ages are defined—in our eyes—by scientific ignorance, technological limitations, irrational superstitions, and political and religious barbarity. Scientific truth, and the humane reasonableness that accompanies a respect for objective facts, has enabled us to discard the superstitions of the previous age and has given us enormous power over nature. This is obviously an improvement on the past. Not only is it an improvement on "our" past; from the colonial age on, the West has seen itself as "advanced" in relation to *all* pre-modern and *all* non-scientifically defined civilizations, in *all* times and places! This high vision of ourselves is what gives Progress its capital "P."

But are we really the pinnacle of all advancement in civilization? In recent times, the idea of Progress has been roundly denounced as culturally hubristic by post-colonial thinkers. We *are* civilizationally different, yet I am inclined to agree with the argument that says "difference" is one thing, but to evaluate that difference as "progress" is another thing altogether.

Actually, I think the way in which our conception of knowledge denies truth to being and belief is a disaster. Here is a short list of problems:
- we can't integrate facts with meanings;
- we have a flatly materialist and pragmatic practice of life, whatever our personal religious beliefs might be;
- power likes to operate outside of morality (we call this "realism");
- morality is separated from legality, and;
- we treat our most existentially significant belief commitments as matters of arbitrary personal preference.

In more general terms, we routinely perform acts of staggering emotional, relational, and spiritual stupidity, simply because we are instrumental scientific realists. We may well end up destroying the fecundity of the biosphere simply because financial and political power is too deeply entrenched in amoral short-sighted pragmatism to take wise account of its own long-term interests. Our strange "realism" is a function of a life-world constructed out of objective facts: quantified, observable, non-qualitative, non-meaningful knowledge. Our fact-defined life-world then constructs an astonishingly bleak cosmology. Here, our cosmos has no transcendent meaning, it is simply "there." Only physical needs and instrumental power are visible to this knowledge vision. So realists amongst us apply themselves to understanding how things in the (meaningless, valueless) cosmos physically work, and then work out how to bend the physical properties of things to whatever use our "factual" needs and wants require. Meaning and value are thus understood as mere constructs of physical use, desire, and power. This feeds into a consumer culture where the only realistic reason anyone does something is to create a market for their narrative of constructed meanings and values in order to sell something and make a profit. Meaning and value are debased to the level of their uses as weapons for gaining a competitive advantage within the categories of commodification, marketing, and personal preference appeal. Ironically, in the end it is only money that has any meaning and value (even though we all know that money is an entirely artificial construct).

I am writing this short book in order to try to uncover the distinctive way in which our conception of valid knowing makes the very idea of "being" incomprehensible, and renders "belief" a matter or arbitrary personal preference. I am doing this because I am convinced that the displacement of premodern conceptions of being and believing by a distinctly modern conception of knowing is bad for us. To say this is not to denigrate modern science and technology. Scientific knowledge provides us with a wonderful window on *certain types* of truth, and our technology has some amazingly good uses. The problems is that modern *scientia* (knowledge, know how) has debased and displaced *sapientia* (wisdom, know why). But it is *not* the case that *scientia* is bad in itself.

The Argument of the Book

The basic idea in the following pages is that being, knowing, and believing always have their meanings in relation to each other. This principle holds true even when one of these terms disappears. That is, "being" is now an idea that has very little meaning to us *because* of how we understand knowing and believing. This is concerning because ideas about fundamental categories are important for our understanding of ourselves and the cosmos in which we live. Without viable primary ideas that relate clearly to our shared experiences of meaning, purpose, and value, we develop cultural blind spots in our capacity to reflect on our experience. When this happens our blind spots lead to an inarticulate meaning deficit in vital areas of our culture, which then shapes the life-world in which we live in inherently inadequate ways. We shall try to put words to these meaning deficits so that they can be brought out of the assumed backdrop of our way of life. The hope is that in articulating some of the foundational premises of our modern life-form, a new range of possibilities for addressing the unsolvable problems of our way of life can come into view. We need to change our way of life at the level of its primary assumptions, rather than just trying harder to solve its existing problems.

Solvable Problems

Because of our understanding of knowledge and belief, and our non-understanding of being, even the simplest problems of essential value, meaning, and transcendence are now unsolvable. We try to construct answers to the wrong problems in the wrong terms. The way we approach suicide in Australia, alas, illustrates this well. But it would be a mistake to maintain that "youth suicide" is an unsolvable problem. Rather, the way we think of the problem makes it unsolvable because we are not seeing the real problem. If we saw the real problem and if we had the will to take actions that were going to address the real drivers of the problem, the problem could well become responsive to our reform efforts.

A hallmark of our times is a certain fatalism born, ironically, of our enormous instrumental power. We often have a civilizational overconfidence in our ability to find a technocratic solution to our "problems." But technology, bureaucracy, management, and financial power all define our "problems" in the value-neutral, instrumental, financialized, and naturalistic terms of the "solutions" they are able to offer. When our "solutions" cause deeper problems or totally fail to address the real existential and spiritual drivers of any given problem, then we think "well, the problem is unsolvable." But it is not the *real* problem that is unsolvable; it is the problem that does not exist—the problem we have defined by our reductively immanent vision of knowledge and our merely instrumental understanding of power—that is unsolvable. The unsolvable problem does not exist because the terms in which we have sought an answer are not true to reality. Understanding our *real* problems, in terms that are appropriate to the nature of the problem, allows for real solutions to our problems. But if we have lost terms that are appropriate to the richly valued, transcendently horizoned, intrinsically significant reality in which we live, then we will not even know where to start understanding what our real problems are, let alone find solutions to them. So the recovery of terms that fit our actual experience of reality is what this little book is advocating.

2

RECOVERING BEING

In the following pages I am going to argue that we often assume very strange and even impossible ideas about what knowledge and belief are. In response to that diagnosis, I will seek to re-define and justify better ways of understanding knowledge and belief, and how they relate to each other. That is going to be a difficult task, but two things help. Firstly, the words "knowledge" and "belief" have an immediate and everyday meaning to us. This gives us a point to start from. Secondly, in recent years a lot of very serious thinking has been done by intelligent people seeking to understand what knowledge, as a feature of our lived reality, actually is. The close relationship between the knowledge of facts and the beliefs and practices of communities, at least at a sociological level, is now pretty well understood.

The word "being," however, is different. For a range of historical reasons, the deeper meanings of "being," which are embedded in the history of Western philosophy and theology, have little connection with our everyday language now. The meaning of "being" has become culturally lost to us.

In general terms, modernity largely sees this loss as a good thing. Modernity often sees itself as a firm progressive rejecter of all things medieval and classical. To modernists, most things pre-modern tend to be horribly embedded in superstition, unprovable speculation, pre-scientific ignorance, oppressive socioeconomic structures, and political and economic repression. "Being" is considered archetypally pre-modern in the above sense. As will become clear, I do not agree with modernity in its disdain for the pre-modern Western tradition concerning being. But whether the loss of that tradition is a good thing or a bad thing, if we do not understand how this loss happened, we are not well positioned to evaluate that loss.

How "Being" Was Lost in the West: The Central Terminological Tangle

I have considerable sympathy with the modern tendency to disdain "being," and its science, ontology. This field of thought had become genuinely dysfunctional by the time modernity emerged from post-Reformation late medieval Europe. Even so, I think a simplified untangling of the basic terminological knot in Western ontology does allow for a good recovery of the classical and medieval traditions of ontological thought, for our times.

The knot mentioned above arises from the late medieval terminological mangle that arises from thinking about "being" in two very different ways. A high medieval and non-Neoplatonist Aristotelian sense of "being" refers to what it is that makes material things (e.g., a tree, a house, a cat, a person) "be" some comprehensible thing in particular. This understanding of "being" produces the science of the substantial manifestation of intelligible things; something preemptive of eighteenth-century empiricism. However, the early medieval theological heritage of that same era used "being" in somewhat Platonist sense (though early medieval Platonism had very little access to Plato's writings) to refer to timeless mental realities that do not materially exist. This was called "Realism," and here, for example, the mathematical idea of the circle is a real being. This understanding of "being" produces a science of pure intellective forms; something preemptive of eighteenth-century rationalism.

Plato and Aristotle both speak of intelligible forms and particular material things, but the relation of form to matter is different between Plato and Aristotle. Plotinus and Aquinas quite viably synthesized those two different approaches, and solved the terminological problems these two traditions give rise to within the Greek and Latin trajectories of Western thought. Yet, from the late thirteenth century on, new ideas entered Western thought about being that made ontological terms intractably tangled. Serious thought about being in the high age of Aristotle—the fourteenth to the seventeenth century—became an arena of acute subtlety and complexity. What seems to have happened is that thought about being became such a thicket of terminological complexity in the late Middle Ages that the seventeenth-century founders of modernity more or less gave up on ontology altogether. Certainly Galileo and Bacon had no interest in "being." In the age of science and technology, *practical* knowledge—knowledge that gives material power—became far more important than abstruse questions concerning the nature and meaning of "being." When eighteenth-century philosophers try to work on rationalist and empiricist views of reality, they do so consciously after the scientific revolution, but it does not seem to me that they succeed in cutting themselves free of the terminological knots in which "being" was already embedded; instead they actually proceeded with the further knot of modern naturalistic reductionism thrown in.

By simplifying and clarifying the basic terms of Western ontology, and by noticing how the discipline itself became a horrible train wreck well before the rise of modernity, I think we will gain an appreciation that the absence of ontology from modernity is *not* simply how things must be, and I believe we will be able to recover classical and medieval ontological insights, for our times.

Let us, then, start at the beginning of the story of "being" in Western thought, and work our way toward its demise in late medievalism.

In the Western philosophical tradition, though about "being" starts with wonder.

Wonder and Philosophy

The Irish philosopher William Desmond, like Aristotle, is very taken with the primal experience that gives rise to philosophy—*wonder*. Desmond calls this primal experience "an original wonder before the given-ness of being."[1] That is, the first "object" of the wonder that is the fountain source of philosophy is what we might call *astonishment with being itself.* Without getting technical about whose understanding of "being" we are drawing on, let us seek to briefly outline what "astonishment with being" is.

To find ourselves as existing, thinking beings, situated in inter-dependent relations with all manner of other beings within a cosmos that hangs together in a meaningful and orderly fashion; this is the primary marvel motivating any sort of sustained thoughtful reflection on the meaning of things. The point of using the word "beings" (things that "are") here is that the wonder that gave rise to Greek philosophical reflection is a response to the revelation that *any*thing "is."

1. Desmond, *The Intimate Strangeness of Being*, 5.

In English the words "being," "is," and the phrase "to be" are all grammatical variations on the same Greek family of words used in ancient times to talk about the "object" of basic wonder; "is-ness." Here "being" is bigger than the particular reality of any given thing, for *"being" is the common property that all things share in virtue of simply being something*. Thought about what "is-ness" is, and reflection on the marvel of there being something rather than nothing is the philosophical discipline called ontology.

The Greek-language origins of "ontology" unpack in the following manner. The "onto" part of the word comes from the Greek *"to on"* or *"to ontos,"* and the "logy" part of the word comes from the Greek *"logos."* The words *"to ontos"* mean "the really real," where *"to on"* means "is" (as distinct from *"me on"* meaning "is not"). The Greek word *"logos"* means, in this context, "reasoning about." Thus, ontology is philosophical thought that concerns itself with understanding the nature of that which truly "is," and, by extension, ontology is the contemplation of "is-ness" itself.

The thing that makes ontology such a demanding discipline from the very outset is that "is-ness" as such is not the same thing as the concrete immediacy of our experience of ourselves, or of any thing in particular. *Why* reality "is" and *what* "is" is are not the same as understanding what any particular thing within reality is.

The Greek Fathers of Ontology: Parmenides, Plato, and Aristotle

The Greek thinker most strongly associated with the pre-classical origins of Western ontology is Parmenides. Parmenides draws the sharpest of lines between the unchanging "is-ness" (*to on*) of that which is really real, and the "not-is-ness" (*me on*) of the shifting world of illusions we call tangible experience. To Parmenides, the apparent and shimmering realm of experience, with its change, plurality, and our unreliable opinions about it, is not real and has no enduring or defined "is-ness." In contrast, the unchangeable and intangible "is-ness" that is accessed by abstract reflection on the nature of what must be in order that what is might be intelligibly grasped, alone is real. That which really "is" is fundamentally simple and does not change, according to Parmenides. That which changes is not actually comprehensibly real, for how can you know something that is not itself from one moment to the next?[2]

2. Parmenides, along with other early Greek philosophers, astutely observed that

It is important to grasp that a key feature of Parmenides' ontology is that only what is genuinely stable (i.e., the eternally unchanging) can be known. That is, in Greek ontological thinking there is a tight relationship, right from the outset, between true *knowledge* and real *being*. This is a profound insight that we shall explore further later.

Let us summarize Parmenides' approach to thinking about being as follows.

> Parmenides' ontology: "being" is that which eternally and unchangingly "is." There is nothing else that really "is," such that the realm of tangible appearances "is not" and cannot be known.

Relegating all of our experience of the world to the category of untrue illusions struck many an ancient Greek (as well, no doubt, as many of us) as making more out of the problem of experiential uncertainty than was really intellectually justified. Yet Parmenides' arguments are by no means facile. It was not until Plato that the difficulties of Parmenides' arguments were powerfully addressed and reformulated.

This leads us on to Plato.

Plato is strongly indebted to Parmenides, but he modifies Parmenides in some crucial regards. Parmenides has a bi-polar understanding of the difference between eternal reality and temporal appearance, such that reality does not tangibly appear, and tangible appearance is not reality. Plato, by contrast, posits the idea of the "in-between" (*metaxu*) realm of sensible appearances and mundane existence, which neither fully "is" (because apparent material things—unlike being itself—become, unbecome, and change) yet also neither fully "is-not" (because the apparent realm *is*, to some extent, intelligible).

It is worth noting that the metaxologically modified "Eleatic" trajectory of "high ontology" that Plato draws on from Parmenides is often wrongly contrasted with the "Ionian" trajectory of Heraclitus, who celebrates the

---

anything in time is continually changing. If something changes then it is not able to be defined in any sure and knowable way because it has no decisive and reliable identity. So only eternal things—things not subject to temporal change—can really have any enduringly true and decisively knowable nature. To Parmenides, anything in time is thus not really itself in any sure or definable way; it has no fixed being. Indeed, to Parmenides, temporal things fail to be anything at all as judged by the only standard of genuine truth—unchanging eternal reality.

flux and contingency of our experiences within existence.[3] This contrast is invalid because it ignores the fact the Heraclitus was a great, possibly the original, Greek thinker of *Logos* (the Greek word for divine, cosmos-ordering reason). The energetic motion of fire, which burns up its material grounds, is placed in wonderful dialogue with a cosmic *Logos* in Heraclitus.[4] Heraclitus teasingly implies a relationship between transcendently grounded meaning in the cosmos and the flux and motion of observable phenomena, but it is Plato who draws this relationship out in understanding phenomena's relation to being via thinking of experience as "neither fully is, nor fully is not" (*metaxu*).

Let us summarize Plato's approach to thinking about being as follows.

Plato's ontology: "being" is that which eternally and unchangingly "is" and only "being" can be really known. Yet "being" is also partially expressed in the realm of material appearance. The realm of material existence is an "in-between" realm that neither "is-not" nor fully "is." Thus, matter and existence participate in being, but matter and existence are derivative and dependent on "being" for the in-between type of reality that they exhibit. Thus, there are two levels of "being": "being proper," which is the realm of eternal and unchanging intelligible realities, and then there is the realm of "particular en-mattered beings," where there is a *degree* of reality and intelligible truth accessible to our existing en-mattered minds.

Interestingly, there is also a third "ontological" level in Plato; the level of reality "beyond being" out of which "being" itself arises. "Being proper" does not generate its own reality. More will be said on Plato's understanding of "the ground of being" later on.

After Plato, the next great Greek thinker of being is Aristotle.

Aristotle takes things a step further away from Parmenides than does Plato—and a step further into ontological complexity—by effectively claiming that there is no realm of "is-ness" that is not also materially apparent, at least as far as our knowledge is concerned. To Aristotle, "is-ness" is always

---

3. In what might be called twentieth-century introductory textbook accounts of the history of early Greek thought, Presocratic thinkers who lived to the West of Athens—"Eleatic" thinkers—are seen as advocates of eternal unchanging being in contrast to Presocratic thinkers who lived to the East of Athens—"Ionian" thinkers—who are seen as advocates of natural processes of continuous change. This characterization is not very helpful as both the "Eleatics" and the "Ionians" are often deeply interested in both change and eternity.

4. See Schindler, "The Community of the One and the Many," 413–48.

"substantial" (to Aristotle, only things of "substance" can "be"). Embedded in this move is a significant break with the priority of the intellective over the material in the ontology of Parmenides and Plato. Even so, Aristotle's understanding of "what really is" is notoriously complicated, and he does contradict himself in various places.[5] It is not fair to Aristotle to locate his contribution to ontology entirely in terms of his doctrine of the unity of matter and form (which is known as hylomorphism) in everything that we can know that "is." But when I speak of Aristotle's distinctive contribution to Western ontology, it is his hylomorphism that I have chiefly in mind.

Let us summarize Aristotle's approach to thinking about being as follows.

> Aristotle's ontology: "being" is that which eternally and unchangeably "is," yet, at least from our perspective, "being" is always expressed in eternal matter and within a dynamic cosmos. There is no (for us, knowable) realm of "being" beyond the realm of en-mattered and temporal existence.

After Aristotle, the meaning of "being" in its classical context becomes, to put it mildly, complex. Things get even more complex in the Middle Ages and beyond. We will now back track a bit and then work our way up to understanding the late medieval tangle.

Western Ontology after the Classical Era

In classical times, the dominant approach to the meaning of "being" was drawn largely from Plato's usage. The Neoplatonist approach to synthesizing Plato and Aristotle placed the learning order priority on Aristotle over Plato (you learn logic, science, and virtue ethics, etc. first), but an interpretive priority on Plato over Aristotle (Plato was considered to have the more profound grasp of higher matters of the two great classical sages). So when the understanding of "being" in Plato's thought was not in harmony with Aristotle's thought regarding the relation of form to matter, Neoplatonism took this approach. Aristotle's hylomorphism was treated very seriously in regard to *material* beings, but hylomorphism was not accept as a valid way

---

5. The apparent incoherence in different sections of Aristotle's understanding of the science of being is probably not the great philosopher's fault, as the text we now call Aristotle's *Metaphysics* was compiled some centuries after Aristotle's death from a bit of a mash of Aristotle's lecture notes.

of understanding the nature of *being itself*, or for understanding the divine grounds of being.[6] Hence, Aristotle's doctrine of hylomorphism, taken as a final ontological outlook (and it is by no means clear that Aristotle took hylomorphism as the final word on ontology), does not have a deep impact on Greco-Roman ontology. It is not until the rise of medieval thinking, when Aristotle was read largely without reference to Plato, that the ontological differences between Plato and Aristotle's hylomorphism become significant in the West. Here terms become very complex.

Thomas Aquinas' brilliant synthesizing mind aims to keep faith with the Christian Platonist ontology of Augustine and Dionysius *and* incorporate Aristotelian "informed materialism" into his philosophical theology at the level of our existence. When, after Thomas, Duns Scotus enters the fray, he inserts stunning anomalies into Christian Platonist ontological categories. In contrast to Plato and his heirs, who distinguished different modes of being (God beyond being; eternal intellective being; the being of the sensible realm that is between being and non-being), Scotus flattens out being in such a way that removes different ontological degrees of reality. This he does by the notion of the so-called "univocity of being." This means that the word "being" has only one meaning. One either has being or one does not. There are no degrees of being. On this view, there is a semantic equivalence in the term "being" when referring to the "being" of God (who is "beyond being" to Plato, Plotinus, and Dionysius) and to the "being" of a pile of horse manure (which is not within being at all for Parmenides). So, the word "being" when applied to God has exactly the same meaning as it has when applied to a chair.

How then is Scotus to preserve God's otherness? He does this through the introduction of the idea of God as an infinite being. But this cuts the nexus between intelligibility and being, for the infinite is not knowable. The intellective essence of any creature, which is partially expressed in the transitory medium of space and time, must be finite—indeed, definite—to impart a partial knowledge of itself, even if only God fully knows what

---

6. As Gerson points out in *Aristotle and Other Platonists*, the Neoplatonist approach to the synthesis of Plato and Aristotle was pretty convincing because there really is a lot of common ground between Plato and Aristotle. Plotinus subordinates Aristotle's hylomorphism to Plato's tripartite conception of the ontological order of reality, but treats hylomorphism at the level of our tangible experience of the world very seriously. Aquinas too, without the aid of Plotinus, argues along similar lines in his affirmation of in-formed matter as being genuinely real, without accepting the idea that matter and form are the co-equal and co-eternal principles of being as such.

the finite essence of any creature is. But God as "infinite being" is utterly unknowable and removed from us because of his infinitude. God becomes an ontological contradiction—a being that is essentially undefined.

Scotus radically discards the Neoplatonist and patristic understandings of being such that a broadly coherent use of terms in Western ontology, which maintains continuity from its Platonic classical origins and into fourteenth-century medieval philosophy and beyond, becomes almost impossible. As mentioned above, I am sure that this late medieval development contributes to the intellectual malaise of late-scholastic ontology such that the ties between metaphysics, theology, and "natural philosophy" (science) become astonishingly complex and abstruse. After the scientific revolution of the seventeenth century, ontological thinking itself becomes in many ways redundant and we now have analytical and materialist thinkers using the term "existence" as equivalent with "to be," which radically derails the meanings of both the ancient and the medieval trajectories.[7]

Let us try to untangle the terminological knot around the word "being" in a little more detail.

Toward Untangling the Terminological Knot

To Plato, only that which is always and unchangeably real, genuinely *is*. Here, if something *is*, it is eternal and universal, and it is always performing the unchanging, unending, and unbeginning action of "being." Thus, what we now call ontology concerns, for Plato, that which really is, *not* that

7. See Brown "The Verb "to be" in Greek Philosophy," 212–37. Brown's chapter is illustrative of what happens when a fine modern scholar reads Plato and Aristotle through the lens of epistemological foundationalism, modern materialism, and British analytic linguistic philosophy. When this happens we are shown a complete unawareness of medieval thought regarding being, existence, and essence, and a profound failure to grasp the undergirding perspective on being shaping the meaning of thought in classical philosophy. Brown has no conception of the intellective and immaterial nature of being explicitly adhered to by Platonic and Neoplatonist thought in antiquity. She makes astonishing claims such as "Why does Plato say the Forms are really real but sensibles not really real? He cannot mean that sensibles do not really exist" (223). Thus, to Brown "The complete 'is' is thought of as the 'is' meaning 'exists'" (214), where "exists" is assumed to mean "sensible material reality." So the distinction between existence and essence in medieval philosophy, the ancient equation of reality with the intellective and the immaterial, and the ancient conception of the partial reality of sensibles entirely escapes Brown in her analysis of the meaning of the classical verb "to be." She gives us a modern linguistic analysis of "to be" in Plato and other ancient thinkers that has *no relation* to the philosophical meanings of classical thought at all!

which is not (about which there can be no reasoning), and *not directly* that which neither fully is nor fully is not—the realm of tangible experience (see *Republic* 477a).

To Plato, real knowledge cannot be concerned with sensible material objects in any primary way, for everything within space and time comes in and goes out of existence and is always changing. Intellection is here a function of mentally apprehending that which unchangeably and universally always is. Being and intellection are profoundly tied in Plato. Thus, the objects of sensory experience—the realm of our material existence—are the objects of "opinion," rather than of knowledge proper.[8] We have a partial "knowledge" of particular spatio-temporal things thanks to the manner in which our capacity for essential intellection is synthesized with our sense experience and common-sense opinion, which is not no knowledge at all, but neither is it stable enough and meaningful enough to attain to genuine knowledge. In contrast, those immaterial intellective truths that have no beginning or end, that are universally the case—such as mathematical truths—really are. Yet any particular, materially existing circle, for example, came into existence and will go out of existence and is not intellectually a perfect circle. No circle we can physically apprehend is "the essential circle," by virtue of the fact of its material instantiation within the medium of flux, transience, and contingency, which is the ever-shifting field of our spatio-temporal existence. But the materially instantiated circle *participates in* the intellectual form of the circle, so we can "know" a circle when we see one for it expresses the form of a circle in space and time, even if that circle only incompletely expresses the timeless being of the idea of the circle itself. Significantly, the intelligibility and meaning of our sensory knowledge is dependent on space and time having a derivative and participative relationship to the timeless mental realities of being.[9]

8. Unlike Aristotle, Plato was not deeply interested in what we now call science, though Plato was very interested in mathematics. Indeed, to Plato, much of what we call scientific facts would not count as knowledge at all, but rather, as (often useful) opinion.

9. The way we might put this in terms of a modern way of thinking about the world is that what we call "natural laws" express the uniform and universal principles describing the necessary relations of matter and energy, where those principles themselves are not matter and energy, but are the timeless (or at least, for-all-time) and spaceless (or at least, expressed-in-all-spaces-of-the-physical-cosmos) intellectual structures of matter and energy. The intellectually apprehensible ideas that govern matter and energy in the physical cosmos are not themselves physical or energetic things—they are a third thing: ideas. If these "ideas" governing space and time were not apprehensible to our minds, we could have no science of nature. Thus, "ideas" are basic to knowledge, and are the very

Aristotle has continuity with Plato in first philosophy,[10] but Aristotle, as mentioned above, makes a notable deviation from Plato concerning the relation of form to matter. For Aristotle is a materialist, but not in the modern sense. That is, to Aristotle matter and form are only ever found (at least by us) together. This means for Aristotle that the form or soul of any given person or being does not survive the deformation of their material body by death or destruction, even though the universal, abstract, and essential Form of Man, which each particular existing man partially embodies, is eternal.[11] That is, to Aristotle, the material and the spiritual are always, and eternally, found together.[12] Consequently, to Aristotle, space and time are as eternal as ideas. To Plato, however, the realm of form is radically prior to the realm of matter. So the sharp distinction Platonic thinking can make between being and existence—where "being" is what spiritually, immaterially, and intellectively timelessly "is," and "existence" is any partial (neither fully is, not fully is not) material instantiation of form in space and time—is quietly but radically defaced by Aristotle. Now only that which has informed material instantiation can "be" to Aristotle. So "substance," the stuff of that which is real, that which performs the act of being, is hylo (wood/matter) morphic (form) to Aristotle; it is always composed of *both* eternal form *and* eternal matter. Being is here made radically existentially temporal and material, whilst also retaining its intellective and eternal essence.

On the relation of form to matter Plato and Aristotle cannot be neatly reconciled. To Plato being is radically intellective, and partial material

---

grounds of the material world.

10. "First philosophy" is thought about that which is essentially and universally real; variously known as theology, metaphysics, and ontology.

11. I'm afraid gender non-inclusive language is native to Aristotle.

12. Anything of form, essence, mind, soul, etc. is "spiritual" or "divine" to both Plato and Aristotle. This is not a supernaturalist understanding of spirit, where a supposedly entirely discrete realm of the divine somehow coexists with an entirely discrete realm of nature. The modern supernaturalist perspective is a function of the sixteenth-century Western doctrine of *natura pura*, and it is entirely foreign to classical thinking. *Natura pura* is the recent theological idea that treats reality as if it is composed of two separate spheres: the "purely natural" material sphere, and the purely spiritual "super-natural" sphere. Significantly, the "natural" and the "supernatural" are now thought of as self-sufficient in relation to each other. Nature no longer depends on the grace of continuous divine providence, such that "natural" things (like thinking) are no longer divinely enabled activities that participate in the divine "super-structure" of an inherently graced and explicitly created cosmos. Thinking, simply because it is done with a physical brain in a material body, is a "purely natural" event to us now; something inconceivable to either Plato or Aristotle.

instantiations of divine essence exist in an "in-between" state, between reality and non-reality, between being and non-being. Thus, our (and all) material existence is also a metaxological (in-between) existence that arises out of being, rather than being an existence of pure matter/immanence, or pure mind/transcendence, or an eternal coeval union of the two.

When Thomas Aquinas gets a hold of Aristotle in the Middle Ages and seeks to synthesize Aristotle's non-Christian hylomorphic philosophy with Christian theology (which is embedded in Augustinian and Dionysian Neoplatonist metaphysics) he undertakes a very complex task. Aquinas sits firmly within patristic orthodoxy in noting that the theology of the incarnation radically glorifies human flesh in a manner totally at odds with a number of middle Platonist, Neoplatonist, and gnostic body-hating trajectories common to the ancient world. Yet Aristotle's apparent rejection of the survival of the soul after the death of the body makes him incompatible with Christian doctrine. To Saint Thomas, Aristotle's astute philosophy does not have all the answers because Aristotle is a pre-Christian pagan trying to understand reality as best as astute reasoning and wise observation allows, without the benefit of Scripture or the action of the Spirit of Truth illuminating the teaching authority of the church. So Thomas modifies Aristotle where his speculations clash with church teaching. The Augustinian Neoplatonist ontological priority of essential form over contingent matter is not frankly denied by Aristotle, but Aristotle's way of thinking does tend in the direction of an inherent and mutual interdependence of matter and form, which Thomas' Christian Neoplatonism and the Christian understanding of the immortality of the soul cannot accept. And yet, the Christian understanding of creation and the incarnation finds strong affinities with Aristotelian natural philosophy, and this Thomas is very happy to highlight. Whilst Thomas affirms "high" ontology and the immortality of the soul, he is also keen to show how the material existence and the spatio-temporal specificity of the actualization of divine essence is basic to the notion of substance and reality as we normally experience it. This is very similar to the trajectory Plotinus followed, even though Plotinus' philosophy is decisively *not* constructed to align with Christian doctrine. To Thomas (and Plotinus) the being of God Himself, in Dionysian manner, is understood only analogically and is emphatically *not* understood directly in the terms of existential reality; "being" as *we* existentially and materially experience it. Thus, the distinctive meaning Aquinas gives to the Latin terms for being, essence, and existence are neither purely Platonic nor purely Aristotelian, they are Thomistic and quite in harmony with Neoplatonist ontology. Let us look at Thomas a bit more closely.

The Latin Move: Thomas on esse (being), essentia (essence), and existere (existence)[13]

To Thomas Aquinas, for any thing within the familiar world of ordinary experience "to be" it is performing the astonishing act of combining a certain distinctive *essence* (intellective "form") with a particular concrete *existence* (things that we commonly speak of existing have a particular location in the realm of matter, duration, and space).[14] Anything that does this action—the actualized and particularized combination of essence and existence—is a being in the material world. So a rock or a person or a tree are all beings that "are" in virtue of actualizing a distinctive intellective form in some sort of duration-limited and spatially defined way, via a particular quantity of matter and energy.

"Form" or "essence" is here understood as much more—but certainly, not less—than what we now think of as structure. The rationally coherent and causally integrated structures of physical reality are an important component of any materially existing being's form, but at a higher, more defining level, form is concerned with the intrinsic *value* (*agathos*), the true *meaning* (*logos*), and the proper *purpose* (*telos*) that is the source of the distinctive intelligibility of any creature.[15] Form concerns that which is *essential* to the intelligible nature of any creature.

Significantly, as modernists, we can now hardly conceive of value, meaning, and purpose as essential features of the reality of anything, let alone of all creatures. Yet, if value, meaning, and purpose are the higher *realities* of intelligible essence—and I shall seek to show that they really

---

13. For the sake of simplicity, I will leave out from this account the important distinctions that Thomas makes between "beings" *entia*, "being" *ens* (that which is), and "being" *esse* (the act of being).

14. At this point I am leaving Thomas' understanding of God and angels out of this account of being.

15. The notion of higher and lower types of forms goes back to Plato's divided line analogy, found near the end of book 6 of *The Republic*. The terms I have placed in parenthesis here are all Greek terms, and not Latin terms, but there is a strong continuity between Thomas and the Augustinian and Dionysian Christian Platonist metaphysics that Thomas adheres to, so I have merged these different linguistic trajectories in order to highlight this continuity.

are—then what counts as "knowledge" in modernity will be radically intellectively defective. More on that later. But here let us note that Thomas' conception of "to be" (the actualized combination of form and matter) has a direct bearing on how he understood knowledge. For, as we have already seen, it is a deep feature of the classical Greek traditions underpinning Thomas that there is a tight relationship between being and knowing, and in that tradition there is an astute awareness that both being and knowing are the stunning primary *mysteries* of our existence. Yet, to Thomas, human knowledge is never pure or complete.

To Aquinas, "pure" essence (form without matter) is, by definition, not found in the realm of material existence. That is, existence is always a partner with essence such that "to be" within existence requires *both* matter *and* form. So "pure" form cannot be fully known or expressed by any existing being, but is only generated and fully known in the immaterial mind of God. Put bluntly, "pure" essence does not exist.[16] But then, pure existence (matter without form) cannot concretely "be" either. So there can "be" no concrete actualization of any "thing" without intellective form, and there can be no merely factual concretion without any ordered and coherent structure to make matter (which is always already formed in some manner) into some particular thing. Thus, every concrete material thing in time and space is dependent not only on its participation in reasoned structures of order, but on particular essential divine gifts, made manifest within existence, to be anything in particular. What we might call material "nature" and intellective "super-nature" are radically integral to Thomas, in good Aristotelian fashion.

Yet Thomas is also a good Augustinian. Hence, the priority of divine donating mind, and the ontological priority of the structure of reason and essence undergirding our material experience of an intelligible world, is upheld by Thomas, and this is a key theological commitment in his ontology.

---

16. Dionysius the Areopagite points out that God—as the creative source of form and matter—does not exist. God is not *an existing being* amongst other existing beings. Hence, pure existence and pure matter do not exist, as both arise from, and are dependent upon, God. What exists is the actualized combination of timeless intellective forms partially, particularly, and uniquely expressed within space, time, matter, and energy. The mystery of the incarnation, then, is that God embodies Godself as a particular man in space and time, becoming a being amongst beings. St. John is suitably staggered that the very Reason (*Logos*) that gives rise to both form and matter in the material cosmos, would become concrete and particular flesh. This is truly the stunning mystery at the heart of Christianity.

This must be carefully noted: Aquinas' Augustinian ontological priority of the intellective over the material is carefully synthesized with his Aristotelian understanding so that "to be" any concrete existing thing, form is actualized in both matter and time. To Thomas, this act, this informed actualization of matter, is what "to be" is for any concrete existing thing. This is not an act any being can chose or fail to do, but it is gifted to every being from the ground of being (i.e., God), which remains ever prior to existing reality itself. So when Thomas talks of "being" as a verb, it is God who does the act of being for every concretely instantiated informed material thing that has existed, that exists, and that will exist. In this ontological way, God is the First Cause of reality, upholding the entire field of being at all times and places, for all beings. This is why there is something rather than nothing. God is the creator of form, matter, energy, and time, and it is God who combines them, calling beings into material existence.

Toward Understanding the Fall of Western Ontology

Thomas does a stunning job of seeking to unite the "high" ontology of patristic theology with Aristotle's informed materialism via the elevation of matter that the incarnation makes possible. However, other powerful minds in medieval times were reading Aristotle differently and were not seeking to synthesize the Platonist ontology of the ancient way with the new knowledge of Aristotle as Thomas was. Most importantly, Duns Scotus introduces two ideas that cut patristic ontology off from the late medieval appropriation of Aristotelian knowledge: God as an "infinite being" and the idea of the "univocity of being."

Before we can examine how incompatible the ideas of "infinite being" and "the univocity of being" are to the patristic heritage of ontology that Thomas adhered to, we need to outline in more detail the tripartite conception of ontology that had been developed by Plotinus and that was largely assumed in patristic theology, and hence, in Aquinas.

Tripartite Ontology

In patristic Christian Platonist ontology, we talk of ourselves as "beings" situated in the "in-between" arena of our historical and material existence, by participation. That is, we can (to some extent) know ourselves and other creatures that exist because intelligible essence makes us and them be something in particular. Essence is the form of any existing thing, and essence gives every existing thing its intellective comprehensible meaning, value, purpose, and nature. It is this essential form that our mind knows, though the means of knowing another spatio-temporal being is always mediated to us via sensation. Without participating in intelligible essence we could not be anything in particular. Indeed, Christian doctrine maintains that the essence of who we are is—as "being" proper is—eternal; our soul is always, unchangeably, and distinctly some intelligible being in particular. But the full being of our soul does not exist within space and time. Rather, our souls, like the intelligible essences of pure being proper, "are," in their essence, in the mind of God. God concretes our soul and calls it into existence by uniting it with matter and the realm of space and time, which God also called into being out of nothing.[17] That is, the form of the basic intelligible structures and also the energetic relations of space, time, and matter, "are" in the mind of God. Christians believe our soul as united with a redeemed body, has an unending existence ahead of it, in the resurrection, but even if it did not, its essence would timelessly "be" in the eternal mind of God, which is the grounds out of which both form a matter are given to be.

So, at the middle level of existence—situated between the (unreal) non-being of "pure" formless matter and the (space-time non-existent) "pure" being of intelligible form—we are beings by participation. In contrast, the level of pure being is the realm of intelligible and qualitative realities that always are, which do not exist in space and time, but which inform existence and enable it "to be" something in particular, by participation.

At the level of the grounds of being itself, God is *prior to and beyond being*, but is more primally real than both pure being and the participatory being of existence. So we can talk of God's "is-ness," God's being, only by analogy, where the terms of that analogy are drawn from our understanding of being. But God's own reality stands ontologically prior to the realm of existence in which we live.

These different ontological categories make sense within a tripartite understanding of ontological hierarchy in these three levels:

---

17. The doctrine of creation *ex nihilo* (out of nothing) preserves the priority of the divine and eternal over the material and transient such as to deny Aristotle's conception of the eternal reality of matter. And yet the material, and material existence, is seen as an expression of the Creator's goodness such that matter is no prison for the soul in Christian Platonism.

1. *Being by participation:* "being," including the existential realm of particular spatio-temporal "beings." This order of "what is" is ontologically derived from, dependent on, and subordinate to

2. *Being proper:* "being," including all the eternal, universal, and qualitative intellective forms, both low and high, that express *Logos* (reason/meaning/order) in the cosmos. (It is divine *Logos* that rationally unifies all things so that there is a universe.) This intelligible order of "what is" is ontologically derived from, dependent on, and subordinate to

3. *Being by analogy:* the "beyond being" of God. God is the source and destiny of all created essence and existence at every level of that which is. God is the true "home" of the *Logos* that is given to being and all beings, and, as such, the *Logos* spoken by God is the fount of all creation, calling "is-ness" out of "not-is-ness" and into both "being by participation" and "being proper." (That is, though "being by participation" is temporal and material, and "being proper" is eternal, both "being by participation" and "being proper" have their origin beyond themselves.)

Here, "being proper" refers to the immaterial intellective and qualitative "grounds" of in-formed material existence. All things that *exist* are dependent upon "being proper" and thus they have a derivative form of being (which is not "being proper," but "becoming and unbecoming"—which neither fully "is" nor fully "is not"), which is what all things that *exist* in space and time do when they perform the act of "being within existence." To state this again, the source of intelligible essence is "being proper" which is not a function of existence. Rather, "being proper" gives reason and quality and intelligible essence to existence. To "being proper" belong ideas, forms, intelligible structures defining universal natural laws, values, meanings, mind, soul, and the divine governing principles of eternal reality; goodness, truth, beauty and unity. "Being by participation" refers to the mode of reality expressed by beings within existence. Here, en-mattered, en-timed, contingently historically situated, finite, particular and culturally embedded concrete beings exist. This is not directly of the realm of "being proper", but is derivative from and participates in "being proper" in order that material things may exist and be what they (becomingly) are for their brief sojourn within space and time. Existing beings are derivative from but not identical with the ontological order of being proper. But, the "ground of being" is God, who is not "a being," and not even "being itself." Though—in like manner to Plato's conception of the goodness beyond being—God is paradoxically partially knowable (analogically) within the field of being and even—in astonishing *kenosis*[18]—within the realm of becoming.

Respecting the three different senses of the meaning of being, as related to different ontological orders of reality, is crucial if the Western heritage of thinking about being is not to become terminologically impossible. Further, within this tripartite outlook, understanding the relationship between "being" and existence is of vital importance if we are to understand the manner in which "being by participation" is a profoundly existential concern, even though "being" itself is not native to existence. But we shall return to existence shortly. For now, let us go back to Duns Scotus and his two astonishing ontological innovations: "infinite being" and the "univocity of being."

The Fall of Western Ontology: "Infinite Being"

To Plotinus—in keeping with Plato's tripartite understanding of ontology—being proper is the realm of timeless intelligible ideas. Being is the source of form in existence, but is not itself native to concrete, contingent, and temporal existence. Being makes material existence intelligible by donating the eternal realities of order, value, and meaning to the realm of material contingency and temporal flux. That is, being donates intelligibility to the realm of existence. Finitude is intrinsic to intelligibility. If some "thing" is infinite, it is not definable in principle, it has no definable nature as such, and hence it is not knowable. Conversely, finitude in Plotinus' ontology means a form is of a distinct and defined nature, such that it can be known. That something can be—to some extent—known, does not, however, imply that we can fully know anything, and indeed perfect essential knowledge is not possible for material beings. This is because an eternal form is never fully expressed in space and time, for space and time is a derivative order of reality that is not fully real. Hence, eternal form is never fully knowable to us as existing spatio-temporal creatures. And yet, for anything to be

18. The New Testament Greek word *kenosis* means something like "self-emptying condescension." It is this word that St. Paul uses in Philippians 2:5b–8. ". . . Christ Jesus: Who, being in the very nature of God, did not consider equality with God something to be grasped, rather, he *emptied* (*ekenōsen*) himself, taking the form of a slave, being made in human likeness. And being found in human form, he humbled himself and became obedient to death; even death on a cross!"

knowable within space and time, there must be a partial revelation of true being (form), and being itself must be finite. In contrast with the finitude and intelligibility essential to the realm of being, in Plotinus, God (the One) is the "ground of being" such that God is *beyond intelligibility*, precisely because God is not "a being," and is not of "being" or dependent on "being," but God is the ineffable and incomprehensible "*ground of* being."

For Scotus to claim that God is an infinite being is to entirely mangle the Neoplatonist way of thinking about the nexus between being and intelligibility, and to render incoherent the Thomistic analogical understanding of the nature of God who is the *ground* of being, but not "a being" as such. There is a degree of conceptual continuity with the analogical understanding of the "beyond being" of God in what Scotus is doing here in regard to upholding the radical otherness of God, for an "infinite being" is indeed incomprehensible. And yet, the reason why Scotus coins this particular way of talking about the otherness of God is that he wants an entirely determinate definition of being itself that applies univocally to chairs, people, ideas, and God. The nexus between being and intellection, between finite form, comprehensibility and definite essence, is radically undercut by Scotus' notion of "infinite being." This entails a complete re-working of the ontological and epistemological heritage from Plato to Aquinas, and is a radical departure from the *via antiqua* way of thinking about both being and knowing.[19]

The Fall of Western Ontology: The "Univocity of Being"

Not only does Scotus want to think of God as an infinite being, Scotus wants to radically flatten out the notion of being itself, undoing the tripartite

---

19. The *via antiqua* means "the way of antiquity," and it is a term that is contrasted with the *via moderna* which means "the way of just now." In the Middle Ages the recovery of Aristotle's writings gave many a scholar great respect for the intellectual achievements of the West's Classical past. Aquinas, for example, did not seek to innovate (even though he was astonishingly innovative), but sought to incorporate the old (Aristotle) with the present (the teachings of the Church). Thus Aquinas situates his own theological philosophy within the *via antiqua* tradition. The modernists—even as far back as Abelard, who also had a great love of Aristotle—sought to surpass the Ancients in order to forge new ways. Abelard did not have access to many ancient texts, but he debunked the "realism" of his day, an outlook that saw itself (wrongly, as it so happens) as loyal to the ancient Platonist traditions of the West.

conception of orders of being in the Platonic ontological tradition. Scotus does this by the notion of the "univocity of being."

For the word "being" to have a clear and stable meaning, so Scotus reasons, it cannot mean something in relation to human beings, another thing in relation eternal ideas, and then another thing in relation to God. The word "being" must have *one* meaning (must be univocal) if we are to use it meaningfully. Scotus is right that there is significant terminological complexity involved in speaking of "being" in three entirely different ways. But rather than generate different terms for "being human," the "being of beauty," and God who is the "ground of being," Scotus obliterates the concept of layered ontological orders in order to have clear linguistic rationality (a very Oxford sort of thing to do). This innovation in thinking of God as an infinite being, and in flattening out the three orders of being into a univocal notion of being, cuts Western ontology off from it Platonic origins. Ironically, trying to demonstrate the existence of God (a horrible mangle of notions for the Christian Platonist tradition), who is now conceived as "a being" within a single frame of reality in which all things (including God) univocally are, is deeply tied to the rise of modern atheism.[20]

The complexities of trying to re-think a recognizably orthodox theology of God within post-Scotist ontology was a task that only the most subtle and speculatively inventive minds were equipped for. The basic insights of Christian Platonist ontology were no longer able to speak to the rarefied logical inventiveness of post-Scotist scholastic philosophy. Throw in William of Ockham's nominalism (this makes the very idea of ontological participation impossible), add the sixteenth-century idea of a sharp division between nature and super-nature such that the proto-modern idea of nature (*natura pura*) needed no donation of divine form to be anything at all, and the very idea of "being" as Greek thought originally found it, simply dies from proto-modern late medieval university learning.[21]

By the time the scientific revolution kicks off, the rejection of Aristotle by the early modernists largely entailed a complete disinterest in ancient ontology in all its forms. In the seventeenth and eighteenth centuries, looking at the world through the lenses of rationalism as "pure thought" and

---

20. See Hart, *The Experience of God* for a beautiful exposition of why modern atheism is irrelevant to an orthodox "ontological" understanding of God.

21. Of course, the Italian Renaissance re-discovery of Plato challenges the dominance of Aristotelian thinking in the late scholastic era, but—as Schmitt in *Aristotle and the Renaissance* well documents—the high age of Aristotle in the West is precisely the period from Ockham to Descartes.

empiricism "as pure experience" entailed a new cosmological vision that was profoundly at odds with a metaxological understanding of our experience of the world where neither thought nor experience could ever be "pure." Further, positing a sharp dualism that separates the univocal practical category of real existence (material reality as "known" by instrumental power) from an entirely supernatural realm of "spirit," rendered meaningless the classical conception of layered ontology in which the ancient idea of being had its conceptual life. For these reasons, the very idea of "being" has made very little sense to the modern world. Yet, "being" has not simply gone away just because the categories of our modern understanding of reality can no longer see being.

After Scotus and Ockham, ontology that is continuous with both the Neoplatonist synthesis of Plato and Aristotle, and with the medieval developments of Thomas becomes increasingly side-lined from mainstream philosophy and theology.[22] In the closing centuries of the Middle Ages, a distinctive form of proto-modern Aristotelianism advanced the notion that knowledge was representational, introducing the subject/object dichotomies that become foundational to modern epistemology, and various subtle varieties of Scotist ontology became lost in the quagmire of quasi-rationalistic theological complexity and volatile ecclesial politics characteristic of late medieval scholasticism. It is, then, no surprise that after the Reformation and the fragmentation of Christendom, Galileo, Descartes, and Bacon make a decisive break with the intellectually moribund and politically dangerous synthesis of ontology and theology that was so opposed to the new ratio-empirical learning they were pioneering. Even so, the loss of the *via antiqua* approach to ontology was, I will now argue, a genuine loss with profoundly impoverishing implications for modern knowledge, belief, and power.

Recovering "Being" for Our Times

The thing that is most strikingly different between a *via antiqua* ontological understanding of being and modern conceptions of reality is that a *via antiqua* ontology is very grounded in our everyday experiences of meaning,

22. Thomas becomes a very significant theologian of the late Middle Ages and of the modern era, but the manner in which Thomas is now read is increasingly at odds with the participationist and analogical ontology Thomas so deeply presupposes in his baptism of Aristotle into Christian theology and philosophy.

value, purpose, and transcendence. These profoundly important features of our actual experience of being in the world are not articulable as features of objective reality to modernity. This puts the modern life-form in the unenviable position of treating reductive abstractions—such as a meaningless sphere of objectivity defined only by quantity, force, and necessary determinate contingencies—as real, and existential realities—such as love, goodness, meaning, divinity, etc.—as unreal subjective constructions.

Appealing to Kierkegaard, I think our metaxological experience of existence makes it clear that value, meaning, purpose, and God are basic realities informing our actual lives, such that a vision of reality that is blind to these primal and all-saturating realities is impossibly disconnected from reality. Further, Kierkegaard is particularly astute in pointing out the manner in which our actual existence cannot be understood in terms of any disembodied, abstract perfection of "pure" mathematical reason or any science of "pure" immediacy and contingency. We live in the existential realm of becoming, which is embedded in the intellective and qualitative realities of being, but existence cannot be reduced to either "pure" immanence or "pure" transcendence. To think we have transcended existence such that we scientifically or intellectually know pure being (essential reality as it really is) or to think that existence makes any sense at all defined in merely quantitative and instrumental terms are equal follies that any three-year-old child is far too existentially present to actuality to believe. And yet, modern rationalism, empiricism, and pragmatism have tried to think of reality itself in hopelessly existentially impossible terms. This false mastery of transcendence, this false reduction of being to "pure" immanence, and this tendency to reduce all meaning to a function of instrumental power all arises because modernity has not had a viable understanding of the relations between matter and form, being and becoming, mind and the unity of the cosmos, from the very outset.

The metaxological realities of our existence require an understanding of the relation between being and becoming, and matter and spirit, to meaningfully connect with our actual experience of being in the world. This intimate connection between being and existence is exactly what is lacking in the modern worldview. The qualitative, sacral, semantic, teleological, ecstatic, and tragic aspects of our concrete existence are strangely outside of the very nature of modern knowledge, power, and objective truth. Modernity is hence strikingly alienated in its basic ideas about reality from the realities of our human existence. This, in particular, is why a recovery of the very idea of being could be such a valuable thing for us today. Let us look a bit more at the relationship between a viable conception of being and the ability to speak meaningfully and act intelligently in relation to our existence.

Being and Existence

Being is the grounds of existence in Platonist thinking. That is, the particular existence of any material thing within space and time is never the cause of its own existence, is always dependent on other things for its existence, and that this thing does actually have its contingent and conditioned journey from non-existence, into existence, and its continuous passage of change until it ceases to exist as a distinct historical thing, cannot be explained by existence itself, and cannot be even understood within the categories of mere spatio-temporality and flux. That is, nothing within the transitory flux of the spatio-temporal field of existence has—"in itself"—any fixed essence that is simply and always there. We do not encounter pure being at all within the categories of existence. And yet, as existing persons we encounter a cosmos in which meaning and reason, order, and purpose, intelligible essence and timeless and universal truths saturate every contingent and fluctuating event and every material thing. This implies a relationship between essential being and existing things. In order to discern the logic of spatio-temporal contingency, in order to "see" change within existence, in order for us to understand true features of movement, and in order for our minds to detect essential meanings partially expressed in that movement, being (intelligible essence) must be the still framework over which becoming (particular spatio-temporal existence) flows. Here being cannot be explained in terms of existence, but existence is inconceivable without being as the ground out of which it arises, and "over" which it moves.

Clearly, the reductive modern visions of a merely material universe of flux "governed" by mindless physical "structures" entangling all events in a great chain of mechanistic contingency is a much less sophisticated outlook than the classical conception of being. Modern naturalistic materialism—which has no conception of any intellective and non-material foundation of being—is also inherently incoherent. For how could there be any order in a realm of true contingency and radical flux, how could our minds discern any timeless or universal principles in nature, and how could we "see" contingency and change if there was nothing non-contingent, intellective, and unchanging undergirding contingency, change, and the order of nature? How could there be an existing material cosmos governed by reasoned universal regularities if mind[23] is not ontologically prior to matter?

The ancient Greek conceptions of the relationship between being/essence and becoming/existence has not been critiqued and found wanting by modern philosophers, rather the modern forgetfulness of being and intelligible essence is a conceptual accident that follows from the seventeenth-century turn to a knowledge of "purely" immanent nature, where "knowledge" is "proven" via an instrumental and repeatable manipulative power over "pure nature." But note, the primal ideas of modernity—a theoretical knowledge of "pure" (entirely immanent) nature, and knowledge as instrumental power over "pure" nature—are abstractions that have no contact with the existential actuality of our lived experience of being human. Modernity has simply ignored being and made it irrelevant to the "pragmatic realism" of the technological society. Modern knowing has excised its understanding of reality from being and as a result the idea categories appropriate to our actual existence have been lost. We have also lost the wonder appropriate to the mystery of existence, for the very categories of thought that modern philosophy wishes to contemplate are bereft of ontological significance. With this loss comes a loss of contact with a source of reality that is intrinsically meaningful and intrinsically prior to ourselves. In this way, the very idea of theology has become obscure to modernity.

A Few Quick Thoughts on Being and Theology

All of the fathers of Western ontology took divinity as foundational when thinking about is-ness. They did this for a persuasive reason. They found that the very idea of *any* sort of meaningful truth about cosmic order required one to reason from a stance of good faith in the reality of divine intelligence that is prior to both the cosmos and our own limited comprehension of meaning and truth. That is, the intelligibility of the world and the truth-carrying capacity of human language and reasoning could only be taken seriously if the world and ourselves were taken as derived features of some transcendent meaning.

This conception of the transcendent divinity of meaning is not a "religious" idea, in the modern sense—it is straightforwardly philosophical,

---

23. In this and similar contexts, by "mind" I refer to God/mind/reason/logos as the undergirding grounds of creation, which is not itself derived from creation.

in the classical sense. Even so, one contemporary thinker who entirely appreciates this "God of the philosophers" is the theoretical cosmologist Paul Davies. Davies has no religious affiliation, yet his stance is remarkably similar to Aristotle's in thinking that mind is prior to our thinking, and that our thoughts are dependent on the real existence of meaning in the cosmos.[24] If we are capable of knowing anything at all, so the ancient fathers of ontology reasoned, this must be because reason is prior to our knowing and our knowing participates in an objective intelligence that is not generated in our own minds.[25] Hence, the rationality and intellectual unity of the cosmos was taken as the *foundation* of meaningful human language, of thought itself, and of all true reasoning and knowledge.

To the ancients, divinity undergirding the cosmos was considered—to use Aristotle's turn of phrase—primitive. That is, the primary reality of divinity is the grounds that makes valid thinking and true observation possible, and as such, this ground cannot be demonstrated by valid thinking and true observation. If one was not prepared to have good faith in the primitive grounds of human intelligence and reasoned observation, then one did not take intelligence, reasoning, observation, and language seriously, and one would not find the very idea of philosophy interesting. So you can see that "faith"—confidence in the divine, primitive, and indemonstrable grounds of (admittedly limited) human reasoning and cosmic order—was considered intimately connected with a valid appreciation of the mystery of being and with the possibility of (partially grasped) true knowledge. One has to trust in and believe in the primitive grounds of human reasoning if one is to reason about an inherently ordered and meaningful cosmos.

Modern philosophy, unlike ancient philosophy, has been obsessed with finding justifications for all the primitive premises of human reason and knowledge. Impossibly, we want rational and empirical justifications for rationality and empirical experience. We have been determined to expunge cosmic good faith and piety toward the divine mind from any claim

24. Davies, *The Mind of God.*

25. *Logos* (meaning, reason), *Nous* (mind) and *telos* (purpose) are fundamental and intelligent ontological realities in which the cosmos is embedded in ancient Greek thinking, realities that make meaningful language, human knowledge, and reasonable and virtuous action all possible. Cosmos-grounding intelligence was the realm of divinity in classical philosophy, whether (Plato) or not (Aristotle) one believed that humans had a personal immortal soul. See Nagel, *Mind and Cosmos* for an interesting look at how an Aristotelian teleological outlook remains eminently sensible today, and how what Nagel—who is without religion—calls the materialist reductionist outlook simply fails to align with our experience of thought, meaning, purpose, and value.

to knowledge and reason that we make. This gives modernity a bizarre affinity with the ancient sophists and skeptics, who were quite peripheral to ancient philosophy. However, they were better than we in following through on the implications of their refusal to believe. For the denial of belief in any primitive premise of the objectivity and goodness of cosmic reason entails the denial of knowledge and truth as well.

Modern philosophy has increasingly come to recognize that the very enterprise of epistemological foundationalism (trying to demonstrate the first principles of true knowledge) cannot succeed. But instead of recovering good *faith* in reason, and instead of abandoning the very ideas of truth and reality, modernity has often sought to define reality in terms of instrumental power and sub-rational pleasure and pain. In other words, that which is primitive to modern philosophy is not order and reason in the cosmos, but meaningless material and instinctive "facts." This leans the modern life-world toward meaningless pragmatism, were purpose is pointlessly defined by non-rational forces. And yet, modernity still likes to think of its scientific knowledge as true, and that reason and order in the cosmos is not just made up inside our own brains. So we are double minded in thinking that objective meaning and cosmos-ordering mind is only a subjective belief, and yet we want our knowledge to be true, our arguments to be meaningful, and theology to have nothing to do with science or philosophy.

The ancients were not like us. The manner in which reasoning and meaning were obviously higher than mere instrumental power and sensible impressions was seen as indicating that mind was ontologically prior to matter. Higher-order realities could not be explained in terms of lower-order realities, in the view of the ancients, though this is exactly the way the reductive mechanistic materialism of modern knowledge approaches such things as human consciousness. This does not mean that higher-order realities (such as the human mind) are not dependent on lower-order material mediums of expression (such as human brains) or that—within the realm of space and time—the materially lower is not temporally prior to the intellectively higher. It simply means that one cannot explain away the higher intellective and qualitative order of reality as a complex function of the lower "merely" material order of reality. But where the qualitatively and intellectively higher is taken as the grounds of meaning and order in the cosmos, no serious outlook on reality can avoid theology.

Space and time are derivative features of reality to any Platonist conception of being, where being is the realm of universal timeless intelligible essence, and becoming is the realm in which such essential realities are astonishingly en-mattered and en-timed, and have a spatially and temporally limited existence as some distinct thing. But material existential "thingness" is not the same as being. Being always escapes the tangibly locatable thingness of any existing thing, though no existing thing can be what it is without an essential form, essential meaning, and essential value donated to it by being. Further, this essence is only ever partially expressed in any given time, place, and contingent context of existence. Existence is a mystery emanating from being, but not traceable back, by us, to being itself. It seems there is another power—beyond both matter and form—that unites them and that calls tangible beings into existence.

Indeed, at the level of first philosophy, Plato speaks of *goodness* as prior to and beyond being (*Republic* 508e) and as the source of all that is, even though goodness is also a form that sits within the realm of being in the same manner in which the sun sits within the realm of the physical cosmos as the source of all life and illumination. By this highest qualitative source of all that really is, which is also the source, further down the ontological ladder, of all that derivatively and partially "is" within the physical cosmos, Plato means *God*.

Augustine, noting the similarities between the revelation of God as "I Am" in the Hebrew Scriptures and Platonist musings about the reality of being, takes being to be God.[26] This move can be terminologically confusing within a Platonist trajectory—how can that which is "beyond being" be "being itself"? But Augustine's understanding of divine being is deeply akin to Plato's understanding of the "goodness beyond being," which is both knowable as the highest being and yet is also the source of all forms, essences, and essential qualitative and meaningful realities that truly are, and is beyond the intelligible essences themselves. Divine reality cannot be said "to be" in the same sense that essential realities are, or even less so in the sense that we are, but as the source of created reality, God is "realer" than reality. That is, reality is itself derived from God. So the divine "being" of God, as the primary "substance" that gives rise to all of reality itself, is often understood as referring to God in early Christian theology, such that the

---

26. On Augustine's take on God as all-present being itself, i.e., as *Ipsum Esse* or *Idipsum Esse*, see Augustine, *De immort. an.* 7, 12; *De lib. arb.* 3, 20–21; *De mor. Eccl.* 1, 14, 24. Cited in Brunn, *St. Augustine: Being and Nothingness*, 101.

Nicene creed talks about the substance of the Son as "of one being with" the Father. Dionysius is clearer and more precise in explaining that the reality of God is beyond our conception of being or reality. Dionysius' outlook is entirely in keeping with the Platonist conception of being and the Hebrew reverence for the mystery of God. In Dionysius' apophatic Christian theology, we see him gesture toward truth and reality beyond conceptual knowing and beyond the very being of the essences that inform matter.

But Christian doctrine is quite breathtaking in its claims about the "*beyond* being" (the unapproachable and unspeakable Yʜwʜ), the "*in* being" (the Logos), and the "*beneath* pure being" (Jesus of Nazareth) of God where only the very highest can also become the very lowest, encompassing and transcending all ontological categories. To Christian faith, the very *Logos* of God became a physical existing person, thus we can in some genuine sense "know" God within the terms of material existence. And yet, God always exceeds the terms not only of human and material existence, but of divine essence (intelligible form) as well. The Christian is able to think of God as the personal source of intellective reality, and, as *Logos* itself, as most fully of the realm of essential being. Even so, because God supersedes the reality of being, we are aware that our knowledge of God is always analogical such that God always exceeds the very possibility of intellective knowledge. So to speak of God as "being itself" is to speak in an analogy that gestures beyond the realm of the intelligible, beyond the realm of being.

The tripartite conception of being in Neoplatonist thinking conceives of the most fundamental component of reality as beyond being, and in irreducibly theological terms. That is, theology is the foundation of philosophy and science in the Neoplatonist conception of ontology that I have outlined above. That modernity typically isolated theology from philosophy and science such that theology is concerned only with the discretely "super-natural," or only with subjective religious beliefs and narratives is a big reason why this sort of thinking is now foreign to us. (When modern theological thinking tries to be "scientific" in modern terms—appealing to notions of objective proof and instrumental effectiveness—it is entirely unrelated to ancient theology. This is as true of "liberal" theology as it is of "fundamentalist" theology in modernity.) But again, this illustrates that our understanding of being, knowing, and believing is always inter-connected.

From Terms and History to Practical "Being" Today

I have thus far sought to untangle the central terminological difficulty that has seeped into Western ontology by reclaiming the tripartite understanding of ontological reality that, I think, is a necessary feature of a coherent Western ontology. But not only is such an exercise in terminological clarification necessary for a coherent ontology, but a coherent ontology is necessary if we are to have a credible understanding of the intelligibility of reality itself, and hence, of our own thoughts. The impossibility of true meaning and the impossibility of gaining an intelligible grasp of truth that so plagues modernity is, I contend, a function of modernity's ontological poverty. Other profound cultural pathologies arise from this poverty too. We have, rather than meaningful and qualitative truth, only instrumental power and quantitative knowledge. Not that instrumental power and quantitative knowledge are bad things, but if that is *all* we have, then there is no reasonable, qualitative, or meaningful purpose (wisdom) to reality toward which our actions—assisted by power and knowledge—should be directed. The "point" of knowledge becomes lost, and the moral direction of power— toward good or bad ends—becomes undecidable. Yet, what modernity likes about instrumental power and quantitative knowledge, shorn of qualitative truth or cosmic meaning, is the "freedom" to *create* meaning and value, out of nothing, for ourselves. In our own eyes at least, we have become "as God," able to generate the knowledge of good and evil for ourselves. Meaning and morality are not truths and realities for us to know, they are projects for us to invent. So free-market liberalism is embedded in a tacitly constructivist conception of meaning and value, premised on the ontological blankness of reality. The manner in which we think about being has a very profound impact on the way we approach actively being in the world. Ontology is a profoundly *practical* matter.

Having retrieved the idea of "being" from its terminological knot, and having located modernity as having been born ontologically poor, let us now look more critically at the modern matrix of relations between being, knowing, and believing.

3

WE FORGET BEING BECAUSE
OF THE WAY WE UNDERSTAND
KNOWING AND BELIEVING

Since late classical times, the West's Christian and pre-modern understanding of three of the most primary verbs of human life—being, knowing, and believing—was typically approached in a decidedly active and integrative manner. But that ancient way—the *via antiqua*—is now foreign to modernity. We have now dis-integrated knowing from believing, and our understanding of knowledge is now typically treated as the passive observation and accurate conceptual mapping of objective facts, and the very idea of being seems strange to us. Today there is a sharp contrast between the integrative, active, and truth-concerned *via antiqua* and the disintegrated, passive, and power-concerned *via moderna*.

Let us briefly outline what being, knowing, and believing are, within a Christian Platonist *via antiqua* outlook, as verbs.

In Greek thinking—and as also found in Thomas Aquinas—"being" is an action. This has been described in the previous chapter, but we can recapitulate the basics here. For us, there are different levels of this action of "being who we are" happening all the time. Firstly, there is essential form being combined with particular matter such that every thing is some knowable thing in particular. This is an action performed by God. But this means that while our "being" draws its timeless intelligible essence from beyond the motion and contingency of existence (i.e., from being proper) and from beyond being itself (i.e., the source of being proper is the mind of God), that essence is always actively outworked in the medium of space and time as long as we are alive as embodied souls. Further, the dynamic nature of this action is not something we simply receive, but within the dynamism of our historical context, we ourselves shape something of who we are becoming. This, for Christian theology, is because we are made in the image of God, with a creative and loving soul. So, within the context of existence, we are gifted by God to become who we essentially are. This process is never completed within existence, but we should asymptote toward our essential perfection when our redeemed eschatological existence is gifted to us.[1] We will return to these matters later, but here all that is needed is the above brief outline of what "being" as a verb means.

Continuing in Thomistic terms for the moment, for anyone "to know" some truth is also an action. To know truth is to exercise the truth-concerned attentions and intentions of the intellect. Here the mind is that which knows, and it knows form, but form embedded in existence. Thus, existence both partially shrouds and analogically reveals essence.

To a Thomistic outlook, knowing is secondarily a function of the passive reception of sensations in the brain through the sensory organs of the body. However, though the site of essence is beyond sensation, this in no way denigrates the body or sensation. For Thomas, as for Aristotle, nothing is known in the intellect that was not mediated to it via the senses. While the senses themselves are passive receivers, yet the mind is an active discerner and interpreter of truth, such that discerning true meaning cannot be reductively defined by the terms of mere sensation. Indeed, as creatures within the created cosmos, the relation of the creature to the Creator is the most primary site of both hermeneutic truth and (should that relation be defective) error.[2]

There is a subtle dialect going on here between all the components of the knowledge matrix: sensation, essential intellective meaning, the primary relation of the soul to God, and the imaginative interpretive processes of the historically and culturally embedded existing knower (the material

---

1. In mathematics, a curve asymptotes toward a definite value when it gets closer and closer to that value, but is said to intersect with that value at infinity. That is, in the sphere of definable mathematical values, the asymptote never reaches the value toward which it is getting ever closer to.

2. See Kierkegaard, *Concluding Unscientific Postscript*. Here Kierkegaard treats sin and faith as the most fundamental epistemological categories.

and temporal specificity of existence). Here the mind does not simply make up meanings and construct "truths" out of the meaningless and merely received materials of sensation. Instead, for Thomas, sensation is the medium of intelligible truths that are given to the mind of the human being, ultimately by God. But the relation between sensation and true meaning is an active process entailing human imagination, and it is a divine-to-human relational process, entailing freedom and creativity, rather than necessity and mechanistic determinacy. To Thomas, the region of freedom—only entered into via right worship—is the first arena of true knowledge.[3] Thus, the relation of the soul to God—a relation of love and trust, or a relation of defiance and distrust—shapes the way we receive and interpret the *Logos* of true meaning more fundamentally than sensation or cultural context.

For Thomas, knowledge is very far from being a merely receptive process. The essential intellective meanings, values, and purposes rightly discerned in the soul of the knower are true meanings, but they are embedded in the sensations and particular cultural contexts and interpretive dynamics of our concrete particular existence. Essence and existence are always entwined for us in such a way that neither pure intellective essence nor merely contingent material existence are fully accessible to the actual reality of our metaxological context.

Knowing is an inherently active process for a number of reasons. Firstly the sensations of existence only ever partially reveal the essential meanings that give form, purpose, and value to any existing being, for form itself is not spatial, temporal, or material. But secondly, existence is always in motion. Hence, there is an active and constructive task required of any given existing mind, the task of imaginatively and analogically discerning real meanings partially manifest in the material medium of flux and contingency.

So knowledge can be more or less true depending on how discerning the imagination of the active knower is. That is, true essence is gifted, partially, to our minds when they are in proper fellowship with the mind of God. The scientist who discerns something about the properties of space

---

3. The notion of "belief" as a free dynamic will be integrated into the notion of knowledge as determinate intelligibility further down the track. Thus, "belief" as truth-revealing is a significant alternative to the modern notion of "proof," which has been so rightly problematized by postmodern critique of modern conceptions of scientific knowledge. Indeed, "belief" that relates in freedom to the divine source of determinate knowledge offers us an approach to truth that neither modernism nor postmodernism can access.

and time does so because in the searching of the human mind for truth, we are in fact searching the mind of God. Or, as Augustine put it, because Christ is the reason and truth of God, whenever we are spoken to by truth and reason in our mind, it is Christ himself, who is our teacher. Knowledge is an active relational dynamic between our mind and the mind of God, and the way we imagine the nature and meaning of truths that condition—but are beyond—"mere" existence, is a creative process in which our conceptualizations reach into the ever-inexhaustible fount of all meaning and truth, God.

Active being and active knowing are also situated within an active understanding of believing for the Christian traditions of the apostolic, patristic, and high medieval times. This is seen very clearly in the manner in which Saint John uses the verb "believe" (*pisteuo*) in his Gospel.

To Saint John, for anyone "to believe" is to express an active confidence in the person in whom one believes. In John's Gospel, to "believe in" Christ has a significant but secondary relation with giving mental consent to a propositional doctrine *about* Christ, it has nothing at all to do with private "belief" conviction that is objectively unprovable, and John did not remotely conceive of belief as a religious freedom within a secular state. No, "believing in" Christ is an active, public, transformative, and existential relationship with the Christ who is the very *Logos* undergirding meaning and true purpose within the entire cosmos, and this relationship with objective meaning and divine purpose entails being drawn into to the very mission of God to the world.

Clearly, thinking of what "being," "knowing," and "believing" mean in the above active terms has very little relation to the dominant contemporary understandings of those three words. Modern English usage tends toward treating "knowing" and "believing" in distinctly *non-active* and *disintegrative* ways. Further, the conception of action modernity adheres to is pragmatically bereft of intrinsic meaning or value. Thus, the notion of "being" as an action hardly makes any sense at all today, as an instrumental understanding of "doing" and of poetically projecting our "own" constructed meanings onto our socially constructed "world" is now central to our understanding of personal identity. So just "being," as some non-pragmatic, non-constructivist enterprise, seems like a passive and empty definitional contrary to active doing and identity making, if it is considered at all. Believing, within the context of a modern liberal understanding of freedom, is often seen as a subjective interpretive gloss or feeling commitment, which should have little if any direct relation to the objective realm of facts and actions at all. Here negative freedom (freedom *from* imposed constraint) is the central issue. We must be free to believe whatever we like about religion, about what products and services we want, and about what values we shall adopt, what moral commitments we will accept, what meanings and aesthetic judgments we find appealing and useful. Whatever we freely choose here is fuel for our personal-identity construction, which does seem to be an *active* sort of enterprise in that we think of ourselves as choosing who we are. And yet because meaning, value, and purpose are themselves understood solipsistically—to maximize negative personal freedom—the activity of personal-identity construction is itself a profoundly internalized "activity." Here we are "active" in our beliefs in the way that shoppers are "active," which is to say that we are largely the passive consumers of things that we did not ourselves make, which other people made for us and tell us we should desire and have, and where the satisfaction of the consumption-based identity experience is an internal satisfaction, readily locked within a narcissistic constructivist virtuality. It is an "activity" that has no genuine traction on external reality. The realm of public action, by contrast, is not seen as a realm of values or meanings, it is a realm of objective facts, of legally regulated behaviors, of instrumental power. So belief is held to be distinct from the public realm of action. The realm of knowledge, too, is itself passive. We think of knowledge as the realm of the factual. Knowledge is simply an accurate reporting of what is objectively, measurably, and predictably the case. So the producer of knowledge is essentially passive, relying on the tools of scientific objectivity to simply measure and record facts, and to discern determinate relationships, which can be harnessed in order to gain manipulative power. Yet knowledge becomes available to action via technology.

The modern life-world presupposes an empty ontology where knowing is a passive recording of mere facts, and where believing is a function of the constructed worlds of values and meanings that populate the private sphere of negative freedom for each individual. The "reality" of modernity is qualitatively and teleologically empty (think of "political realism") where value and meaning have no substantive reality. Here knowledge is of ontologically meaningless facts, and power (the technological application of knowledge) is directed by "factual" but in-themselves-meaningless brute givens (biological necessity, sub-rational desires). It is all profoundly out of touch with the richly qualitative and substantively meaningful reality in which we actually live. Central to the question of why we accept such a life-form at all is the very way in which we conceive of what being, knowing, and believing are. Let us try on a different outlook. Let us ask, what might it mean for us today to recover thinking of being, knowing, and believing as *verbs*, as the ancients did?

Let us look at being first.

What Is Being as an Action?

As we have already touched on, the idea of being as a verb in the *via antiqua* is both profound and complex. Here, nothing that we can tangibly experience purely exemplifies being, but all the things that exist in time and matter participate in essential reality (that which truly "is") in order for matter to have form. Sliding slightly away from Thomas and toward Plato, the ancient outlook on being holds that as matter must have form, hence all things that exist are participatorily related to that which essentially and really "is"; that is, the realm of form. Here anything that exists in space and time only "is" to some degree. This is because existence as we spatio-temporally experience it is not a pure expression of being, but rather of becoming and un-becoming. Thus, there is typically a sliding scale, a moving ratio, whereby the more pure an essence anything in space and time expresses, the less concrete an existence it has. Which is to say that a Christian Platonist understanding of "is" is very high. Something only purely "is" if it is never becoming or unbecoming, but is eternally and unchangeably itself. What this means is that immaterial universal thoughts—which are the world-ordering "words" of the divine Logos, which give form to matter and meaning to reality—are seen as expressing essences which belong to the realm of immaterial timeless "is-ness" proper, and spatio-temporal particular material things express concrete existences as is appropriate to the realm of becoming and unbecoming.

For an example that we have already used, the mathematical relationship between the circumference and the radius of a circle can be said to "be" in this high manner, but no existing circle embedded in space and time is eternal and hence essentially round. Even so, every imperfect circle that does come into and go out of existence in space and time, must, to some extent, participate in the "is-ness," the unchanging essence, the being, of the eternal, non-spatial, non-temporal circle (the divine-word "circle").

So the tension between timeless essential meanings and the dynamic, particular, en-mattered expressions of form makes "being" an action in relation to how we experience it. This action is easier the lower the particular thing is, in terms of its participation in the divine nature. For a rock to be is easier than for a person to be, because the rock has no responsibility for how its essential nature is expressed in space and time. By the laws of physics and chemistry (the form given by the Word of God to the rock), within the context of the specific conditions of space and time it is thrust into, it simply undergoes the act of being for the duration of becoming that is its lot. Yet, there is also a tension between nothing and something inherent in the act of being the rock performs,[4] for the rock's act of being is also an act in relation to existence itself. Where matter itself is not its own grounds—within the doctrine of creation *ex nihilo*—the mystery of particular concretion is as high as the timeless marvel of form. God actively makes the rock "be" within space and time, which God also makes "be" (as distinct from "not be"), by the power of God's divine creative Word (. . . and God said, "let there be . . ."). So all that exists and all timeless essences are not grounded in themselves, but are grounded *in God*, who is the ground of all beings, all matter, and all form, the source and destiny of all creation that "is." To be, then, is to receive the primal ongoing action of God that makes creation exist, out of nothing. This is not a simple process.

The Greeks, starting with Heraclitus, noticed that nothing we experience within our existence is ever stably (that is eternally and unchangingly) simply what it is. Here there is a complex dialectic relationship between essential meanings (*Logos*, Word) and particular changing things. So that which *existentially* "is" is not identical with that which *essentially* "is," even though, to our mode of existence, we never encounter essence that is not mediated to us via existence. For while concrete actuality is only given to that which exists, and that which exists is only comprehensible because it participates in essential meanings (hence, existence displays a mode of "is-ness" unique to the spatio-temporal context of creation), there is a different mode of "is-ness" appropriate to the non-material, non-temporal realities accessible to thought. In terms the Christian tradition is more familiar with, the intellectual is the spiritual. The Greeks in Plato's trajectory believed in

4. "Performs" in an utterly passive sense, being the subject of the divinely determined act of bringing it into existence. All creatures are recipients of a divine action, but part of that action is the ongoing capacity to continuously realize existence (within finite spatio-temporal limits) and this then—in a derivative sense—is an action performed by any existing thing.

the priority of thought/spirit/mind/person over matter, such that the realm of existence is dependent upon the realm of essence, whereas the immaterial intellectual realm of essence is not dependent on the realm of existence. And yet, for us (spatio-temporal beings as we are), our only contact with essential being is *always* mediated to us by the existential context of our actual experience of being alive in the world.

So attempting to understand that which "is" is a complex task. We must approach this task via existence, though essential reality is never reducible to the categories of time and space, which are basic to the realm of existence. Then again, the mystery of existing things "being" something rather than nothing—that existing things have the mode of "is-ness" appropriate to space and time—is also a true object of ontological contemplation.

So, in existential terms, thinking about what it means for us and material reality to be is never ontologically pure. Being and becoming are inseparable within our mode of existence, such that it is legitimate to think of the ontology of existence. Yet, as hopefully clarified in chapter 1, we are actually talking about two distinct intellectual enterprises when we seek to understand the ontology of intellective essences via abstracted imagination, and when we seek to understand the ontology of essence embedded partially—which is to say, dynamically—in existence.

Thus, when I speak in this book of being as an action people are caught up in, I speak of *existentially embedded* being and understand the action of that mode of being in three ways. Firstly, there is the action of God making me "be" as opposed to not be. Secondly, there is the directionally undefined and unconscious action of dynamically engaging my timeless essence with the context of material change.[5] Thirdly, there is the *desiring* and *directional* action of seeking to rightly uncover the truth of my God-given essence (my spirit) within the dynamism of existence, as a continuous journey of the soul into the unfathomable heart of God. This is being as an action.

What Is Knowing as an Action?

Where being (is-ness) is understood as not its own grounds, but as grounded in the source of both form and matter—that is, God—then the cosmos is

---

5. What I mean by "directionally undefined" here is that as persons we have some genuine freedom to choose how we express our essence within existence; we can choose to express ourselves with the grain of our distinctive created essence, or, in some measure, against that grain.

unified at, by, and in its source. This makes the universe a unity and knowledge within the universe *relational* between the parts of a whole, every part of which exists by virtue of its participation in the gift of existence by God. That we now typically do not think like this usually implies that we suppose that both matter and form are somehow their own existential grounds, and that each thing that "is" is discrete and finally alone in its being. This existentially self-grounding and ontologically atomic understanding of being makes the ideas of universe and cosmos inherently problematic, and makes the "center" of knowing only the individual mind of an atomic "I." Thus, the "I" of the non-unifiable cosmos is like a discrete "subject" that peers out onto the otherness of "objects" and then organizes the inputs received in subjectivity so as to try to map and master an objectivity that is essentially "other" than one's knowledge within subjectivity. To cheekily paraphrase Marx, this is "man" squatting outside of reality and peering in.[6] This peering ego knows things within the givens of the ordering structure of the mind by which the inputs of experience are given the semblance of an objective world of things. If we hold that only particular material things exist, and that the organization and reality of matter that defines the existing thing is a brute fact that needs no explanation or grounding beyond itself, then value, purpose, and meaning are understood as subjective glosses, and not functions of objective reality. So knowledge is about the factual mapping of the impressions of objective things, which is an essentially passive process. It is not a process of intention or of mutually active relations between ontologically bonded beings within a participatory ontology.

Conversely, where participatory ontology is assumed, and where a doxological telos for the cosmos as a whole is assumed, then knowledge is active in both intention and in its relational mutuality between the knower and the being that is known. How it would be possible to think of reality at all without such an ontology (for there can be no unity to the universe) I cannot see. So it is not surprising that in classical and medieval thought realism is a function of participatory ontology, and that modernity only understands knowledge in terms of instrumental constructivism. There can be no reality, no realism, in modern knowledge.[7]

6. See Marx, *Introduction to a Contribution to the Critique of Hegel's Philosophy of Right*: ". . . man is no abstract being squatting outside the world."

7. It is a great and characteristic confusion for modernists to think of themselves as realists. By "realism" modernity means a belief that knowledge only exists within our skulls, and that what we have knowledge of is entirely objective, and merely there—with no value or meaning existing in reality, and no unifying divine mind ordering reality into

So let us think of knowledge from within an ontology of participation. Here there is an "objective" meaning, value, and purpose gifted to all beings by the Creator, whether I "subjectively" appreciate it or not. Here all beings are in communion with each other by virtue of each being being grounded in the ground of being, God. When I experience a tree, this cannot be adequately understood as a function of an atomic ego's subjectivity ordering sensory impressions, which are then habitually assumed to correspond to objects independent of my consciousness. No; firstly, the "I" of participatory ontology is not solitary. The clouds, the tree, the table, the people passing me as I tap on my computer in the park—we are all beings within existence, we are all participants in being; they are not discrete objects separate from me, and I alone am the observing subject of my own consciousness. Secondly, as grounded in God, the source of both matter and form is—in Kierkegaard's turn of phrase—the power that establishes the knowing self.[8] Here my mind participates in the very mind of God when it thinks truly, for the meaning and truth of reality is independent of my mind, but it is a function of God's mind. My communion with God at the core of my mind, at the origin of my own thoughts, makes it possible for me to understand objective truth (truth independent of my mind) concerning the created cosmos.[9] So the intentionality of my thoughts—toward or away from communion with God—determine whether my thoughts lead toward truth or toward delusion. True knowledge must be doxologically active.[10] Thirdly, there is the doxological telos of creation itself. I am unified with the tree and the clouds and the other people in the park by virtue of being a creature. All creatures are in communion with all other creatures by virtue

---

a meaningful unity. This cannot be realism, for there can be no meaningful or unified reality to know and even the question of what a knower is becomes meaningless via this set of epistemic and metaphysical commitments. Modern "realism" is actually solipsistic constructivism that incoherently asserts that this outlook is the only realistic way of thinking about what our sensory experiences really are.

8. Kierkegaard, *Sickness Unto Death*, 14.

9. See Augustine, *The Teacher*.

10. In this context, there is an equivalence between an intentionality toward communion with God and an intentionality toward truth (true reality). So the atheist who professes doctrinal disbelief in God may have the intention to understand the truth of what is going on in, say, US presidential politics, and even though it is very hard to get to the truth there, this intention makes the seeker open to the epistemic grace of God such that a measure of truth can be known, whether or not the atheist professes to believe in "the existence of God." To hold truth above power and interest is a doxological act, as Plato points out in book 1 of *The Republic*.

of their common grounding in the Creator. Creation finds its *telos* in the fellowship of love with other beings, and, most basically, with its Creator (worship).[11] That is, purpose and meaning are as much an objective reality as matter and form, but I can only appreciate them aright if I am in a constructive doxological relationship with God, self, and other creatures. Hence, in classical and medieval times contemplation as worship was the basic requirement for an appreciation of right knowledge, for a right appraisal of meaning, value, and purpose, and for a proper understanding of the moral implications of the various possibilities of action that knowledge affords. Here true knowledge is a very active function of right worship.

What Is Believing as an Action?

In John's Gospel, the Greek word *pisteuō* (believe), in various forms, occurs ninety-eight times, and it is a verb. *Pist-* stem words—words we would translate in English as various grammatical forms of "faith" (noun) and "belief" (verb)—were in common use in the marketplace in classical times. *Pist-* stem words had their everyday meaning within the context of what we might now call business confidence, which is the active transactional trust that is a function of proven good will. So public relationships that you can rely on are the grounds out of which *pist-* stem words draw their meanings. Confidence (a word of Latin origin where *con* means "with" and *fide* means "faith") is still used today as a reflection of marketplace trust, even though it is now largely abstracted from the concrete relational terms of good will that older trading relationships relied upon.

The thing to note is that here belief is not a function of personal subjective valuations over which the atomic "I" alone exercises its unrestrained freedom of will in designating credence. Rather, belief is always a relational, public, and practical concern in this older world. And it is a term of action. Indeed, in John's Gospel the *work* that God requires is "belief" (John 6:29). John's Gospel locates "belief" as an active work, a work of *confidence in* Christ that must be lived out.

To *believe in*—verb—Jesus Christ is a doxological, a moral, and a political activity. As the Gospels outline, the *euangelion* (good news) is a proclamation of the reign of God, and those who proclaim it do so in word and

11. Leviticus 19:18b, ". . .you shall love your neighbor as yourself." Deuteronomy 6:5, "You shall love the Lord your God with all your heart, and with all your soul, and with all your might" (RSV).

deed; belief is lived out as life under the Lordship of Christ. This is a total lordship, not a discrete and private personal affair, as seen, for example, in the gnosis of private-salvation cults. That is, to believe that "Jesus is Lord" is to civically disbelieve that "Caesar is Lord" in the public realm. Belief was then—and actually is equally now—highly political. The Lordship of Caesar was vital to the public cultus of the Roman Empire. Challenging the lordship of Caesar was basic to Christian belief (Christians were not killed in Roman arenas for no reason), so the integration of the religious with the political, and the life-form implications of the action of belief were seen as inextricable from the Christian gospel.

Today in the dominant secular West, things are very different. Because we live in a life-form functionally bifurcated into a world of objective facts and instrumental power on the one hand, and subjective meanings, values, and convictions on the other hand, belief has become a function of discretely personal and subjective conviction. Belief is thus not a realm where the objective notions of factually true and false or public power have any purchase. While we may now "believe" whatever we like about spiritualized ultimate concerns and anything to do with personalized significance and private morality, the public necessities of fact and action are carefully demarcated from the private freedoms of personal conviction.[12]

Within our life-form there is a broadly assumed metanarrative as to how our way of demarcating personal belief from the realm of public power arose, and why it is such a good and humane idea. The dominant story about the liberal secular West is one of liberation from the tyranny and violation of bringing public violent power to bear on the beliefs and personal moralities of heterodox non-conformists. We no longer burn or drown witches, heretics, gays, Anabaptists, etc.; we no longer allow pogroms against Jews or religious minorities, etc. We now tolerate all personal convictions and private moralities, provided people uphold the legally regulated public order. In short, belief has had its public teeth pulled and is now a safe jelly-sucking pet that stays firmly inside the realm of private property and no longer goes on bloody rampages through the streets.

12. When beliefs are subjective glosses on objective facts, then beliefs are internalized and de-verbized. Beliefs are now—indeed—constructs, but as inner glosses they are quarantined from the world of "realist" action. They are not verbs in relation to action in the real world. To think of beliefs as real verbs, as actions of interpretive engagement with the real world, there must be a nexus between existentially subjectively appropriated values, meanings, and transcendentals, and objective reality. The absence of that nexus makes belief a mere internal gloss within modern constructivism.

Undoubtedly, violent atrocities against belief non-conformists are a function of barbaric inhumanity. But the idea that the liberal secular West is no longer subject to barbaric inhumanity and violent atrocity, because it is liberal, secular, and democratic, is completely false. Today, policing and warfare—where the power of violence is handed over to the Hobbesian security state—has never been more destructively capable and surveillance invasive, and the off-shore systemic oppression that supports the luxuries of the West—such as the highly toxic "backyard" recycling of computer components in China, Indian, and in Africa, and the integration of tax evasion into normal transnational finance[13]—is conveniently out of sight, but has been a bed-rock of Western civilization's wealth and power ever since Christopher Columbus went to America.

The idea that public power is not embedded in common belief conformity is an astonishing fiction. Liberal secularism is itself a violent regulator of "private" belief. You can believe whatever you like, *provided* you do not believe that your personal beliefs are actually objectively true, or matter in any public way. You can have whatever personal loyalties you like, *provided* you give uncompromising public loyalty to the state in which you are born, to the liberal and secular laws it mandates, and (in the age of heightened security, increasingly unconditionally) accept its total power over coercive violence. So in reality, we have *a single public cultus*, and private cultus pluralism, but our Caesar is now global corporate and geo-political power and our public religion—that which binds society together at its most basic belief and practice nexus—is now a combination of personal salvation via consumption and self-construction, romantic nationalism, and brutal global corporate survivalism, where superrich corporate megafauna exploit unfair transnational advantage at every turn.

I have outlined the above privatization and subjectification of belief in very stark lines in order to clarify the manner in which belief is not understood as a verb that functions in public space within our life-form, but I appreciate that the situation is more subtle. Notably, liberal democracy thinks of the public square as an arena of persuasion, rather than of force, and politics is meant to be a forum where public persuasion is transformed into laws that the people who are governed decide for themselves by democratic vote (as facilitated by representative mechanisms). So our laws are meant to be about justice and community-affirmed values, and the public forum is not isolated from people's deepest personal convictions. However,

13. Cobbing, "Toxic Tech: Not in Our Backyard"; Shaxson, *Treasure Islands*.

the reality is different. Because the realm of objectivity is tightly conceptually tied to mere facticity and mere instrumental efficacy, technology has increasingly displaced humanity in the arena of public power. The technologies of public-opinion manipulation that the mass media uses, and that politicians seek to harness, and that large corporations use with their staggeringly large lobbying, advertising, legal, and accounting budgets, makes the public square anything but a realm that reflects the religious or moral values, or even the actual workplace and economic interests of the people that democratic government is meant to represent. So in reality, the crossover from non-coerced personal beliefs into the public realm of civic debate and legal construction is powerfully shaped by the supposedly merely efficient and merely factual forces of what are in fact highly interested and personally invasive political technologies. Our supposedly personal beliefs and values are relentlessly disciplined by advertising so as to promote an atomic self with our desires always directed toward personal satisfaction via must-have goods and services, and the financial means of attaining them. In reality, there are no hard boundaries between the personal and the public, but we are fed a relentless solipsistic diet of myths and illusions such that our self is radically de-politicized and beliefs concerning all matters of final significance are radically interiorized and made passive in relation to the world we inhabit.

To think of belief as a verb that functions in the public arena is now made almost impossible by the norms and power structures of our prevailing life-world. But an interiorized privatized belief is consistent with the conception of knowledge as merely objective facticity and the forgetfulness of being.

The most significant consequences of this thrice-passive forgetfulness of being, objectification of knowledge, and internalization of belief is that the only things we take to be real are objective facts and mathematically necessary logic that are meaningless and valueless in the common pragmatic reckoning of the "realism" of our day. Ironically, this means that we do not believe (in an active and public sense) what we existentially know to be true as a direct function or our actual experience of being.

On Not Believing What We Know To Be True

Because of the way in which being, knowing, and believing are conceived of and embedded in the life-world practices in which we live, we do not really believe what we know to be true about being. In fact, we believe in what we know is not true, both about being and about reality in general.

Three grounds of our own existence that we have immediate existential knowledge of—knowledge that is the grounds of all meaningful truths—are the meaning of language, the reality of love, and the uncontainable in-breaking of the noumenal. Yet the reflexes of the tacitly materialist and instrumentalist metaphysics of the modern life-form do not treat meaning, love, and the un-masterable being of the real as the foundation of truth. Rather, we treat meaningless facts, loveless logic, and mere instrumental effectiveness as the grounds of a valid knowledge of reality. That is, we treat that which we existentially know is a construction of our own mental reductions and abstractions, and that which we know is a mere tool of instrumental will, as real. And we treat that which we existentially know to be real as—at best—apophatic, as unsayable surds of impenetrable transcendence that we keep separate from the (supposed) world of factual knowledge and instrumental power. If only we would believe what we know to be true and disbelieve what we know to be abstract, reductive, instrumental constructs.

Let us look briefly at the above three existentially grounding realities that we know are true, but do not actively and collectively believe in.

The Meaning of Language

Language is the medium of meaning and the reality of meaning is tacit in all language. This reality cannot be reduced to mere instrumentality or as personal or collective or artificially imposed mental superstructures constructed over the top of meaningless facticity. In Christian Platonist terms, *Logos* is a fundamental premise of reality as it is given to our existence. *Logos*—the meaningful nature of creation—is the grounds of all language; be it human, animal, biochemical, or mineral. We are embedded in language from before we can talk as it is the pre-verbal intrinsic meaning of reality out of which verbal and mathematical language arises. The intelligence of a newborn child is astonishing. We are beings equipped to receive, appreciate, and non-fundamentally generate meaning from the very beginning. Meanings ground our existence because *existence is within meaning*.

Logos—the "words" that we understand when we are grasped by the manner in which reality is grounded in meaning—speaks of the divine mind who speaks reality into being, who gives form to matter, who embeds purpose, intention, order, goodness, and joy into the very fabric of all that exists. Thus, God is the most fundamental reality known to our existence as linguistic beings. We can say that we do not know God, but this is an inherently incoherent statement that denies the grounds of meaning in reality itself. To disbelieve in God is to (negatively) believe something we know is not true. To disbelieve in the already-meaningful nature of reality—a meaning prior to the intrinsically analogical and imaginatively hermeneutic enterprise of human linguistic expression—is to deny the meaning of language as such. This cannot be done without cutting off the branch one is sitting in intending to speak meaningfully.

We know language is meaningful. We know Logos gives meaning to the reality in which our existence is grounded. We know God speaks meaning into reality. We cannot existentially renounce the meaning of language and the meaning of reality, whatever we might say we believe. Yet we do not make what we know to be true the grounds of our beliefs and actions in the life-world of modern consumer society. And there is an obvious reasons for this. The life-world of modern consumer society is not grounded in reality. We will return to this later.

The Reality of Love

As Martin Buber has pointed out, one's sense of "I" is located, from the very beginning, in relation to the "Thou" of the primary carer of the child just born.[14] Indeed, this relationality is prior to birth where, in utero, it is the most physically intimate experience of dependent relationality we will ever know. The sense of I at all, and then the sense of I-at-some-distance-from-Thou, and then the sense of I-as-in-some-sense-independent-of-Thou, comes much later, but it never escapes its relation to Thou as it is derived from an initial undifferentiated matrix of common life between mother and child.

Human beings do not live as infants if they are not cared for, if they are not recipients of love. Deficiencies in the experience of being loved and cared for in infancy are profoundly psychologically scaring. In this sense, the experience of love is a primal existential reality that we all know is basic to our very identities as "I's." It is true that varying degrees of personal insecurity and anxiety about the validity of one's ego, as situated in agonistically or hubristically displayed relational reflections, are also universal experiences. But if love is *real*, these aberrations are not positive realities, they are

14. Buber, *I and Thou*, 40–44.

shadow sides, absences, that indicate the primary reality of love. Could it be that the primary reality of love is indicative of the objective reality of the good in which our existence is situated?

The question of whether love is a primal feature of reality or merely a derivative feature of human relational dependence cannot be meaningfully separated from the hermeneutically prior cosmological assumptions through which one interprets the difference between the primary and the derivative. We will here only briefly touch on the two dominant cosmological trajectories within Western culture since Augustine: human nature and the cosmos are both fundamentally competitive (human love is a derivative function of self-interest), and human nature and the cosmos are both fundamentally harmonious (Love itself is a primary reality).[15]

The experience of evil and arbitrary destruction is *only problematic* if an ontology of cosmic providence is assumed. Without such an ontological framework, evil simply is, and is not a problem. That we cannot actually experience evil without it being problematic to us naturally leans us toward an existential belief in cosmic providence as an eschatological hope, and as an anguished cry of dissatisfaction in the oversight of providence now, and as the reality to which we address our laments concerning the wrongness of injustice. Of course, there is no necessary abstract logical tie between our experience of evil as problematic and the reality of primal cosmic goodness, but I am not here interested in abstract rational possibilities, but in concrete existential actualities.

In Augustine's understanding of original cosmic harmony and of the primal transcendent goodness undergirding creation, evil is the shadow, the privation of good, it is not some positive qualitative reality in its own right. Goodness could exist without evil, but evil could not exist without a derivative and privative relation to good. What we might call arbitrary amoralism—where things just are how they are, with no qualitative attributes—is abstractly conceptually possible, but as noted above, such a stance has no real relation to the texture of our actual existence. When we and those we love flourish, this we experience as good, when we and those we love are frustrated, exploited, snuffed out, this we experience as bad or evil.

15. It is an intriguing fact that both of these trajectories in Western culture have their post-classical origins in Augustine. For Augustine upholds both that goodness is primal to creation, and that original sin is now within us all. For a very interesting look at the impact of Augustine's doctrine of original sin on Western culture from the late classical era to the present, see Boyce, *Born Bad*. For a fine exposition of Augustine's understanding of original harmony, see Dueweke "The Augustinian Theme of Harmony."

The alternative cosmic narrative to cosmic providence sees the struggle for survival and original contest as primary. Here love is seen as an instinctive necessity that serves survival, but is of no primary significance. Here survival and dominance are seen as good; here there is a moralism in being ruthlessly dominant, and an immorality to being weak, dependent, and dominated. Indeed, this narrative is the preferred narrative of our own agonistic, competitive, instrumentalized culture of conquest, just as it was of many an ancient warrior culture and cultus (such as the cultus of Marduk in ancient Babylon). The CEO instrumentally uses the staff of a company to maximize short-term profitability so as to succeed in the dominance contest of the market place, which the CEO uses to promote (usually) his own career advancement. Egotistic instrumentalism in a callously agonistic cosmos is assumed here. Jon Ronson's fascinating book *The Psychopathy Test* explores the dynamic of the frequency of clinical psychopathy in senior management circles. Our high-flying corporate, financial, and political culture lauds the morality of the psychopath because this is seen as objectively "realistic" and a reflection of what everyone would like to be if they could. But this is not the case. The morality of survivalism is not how most normal people really live and has a distinctive genealogy in modern times. Yet this "morality" has had a long lodging in Western high culture.

Francis Bacon's determination to make instrumental power the center of Western learning was naturally suited to a civilization bent on conquest. The Royal Society for the Advancement of Science was patronized by the aristocracy (not the university), not because the new mathematico-experimental method had an objective interest in truth, but because of what wonderful use the new knowledge had in military application, wealth production enterprises, and the conquest of nature. The new knowledge was for men of action. The age-old attempt to overcome the limits of mortality by making a name for oneself, as expressed so poignantly in Homer's *Illiad*, has always been a deep driver in the ambitious. The ambitious—and who does not know the attraction of ambition?—are deeply invested in seeing the world as a theatre in which others can admire their potent actions and grand achievements.

Augustine's critique of the Western hunger for personal glory has never gone out of date. In the *City of God* Augustine observes that the placing of the self at the center of the matrix of life-form worship practices is "natural," and the dynamics of instrumental exploitation and the abuse of power are naturally a function of human society embedded in this doxological center. But such "natural normality" is itself parasitic on goodness, it is not a self-standing center of its own morality.

This tension between the foundational essential goodness undergirding reality, and the naturalness of human evil and the tragic natural features of death, war, atrocity, disease, and disaster, is expressed in the Christian doctrine of the fall.[16] The fall does not negate original goodness undergirding created being, but it does account for the tragic inner momentum toward the frustration of the primal ontic *telos* of harmony and goodness for which created reality was called into being. We now tend naturally toward that which will not enable the expression of the essential goodness that grounds our own being, and so, to some extent, does all of creation. Creation, so Saint Paul says, groans as it waits for its full redemption, which will be the final eschatological fulfillment of the work of Christ in the world. Even so, the travail only makes sense as a travail, rather than as a simple brute positivism of meaningless suffering, because the Edenic memory and the eschatological hope are embedded in the very fabric of our existence in the fallen present.

16. I am here assuming a distinction between the catholic (universal) Christian doctrine of the fall and Augustine's understanding of original sin. This matter is complex. On the nature and meaning of Adam's sin, I am more inclined toward Orthodox and Celtic readings than the post-Augustinian Western tradition, but the Western tradition is complex and cannot be fairly read as simply opposed to Eastern Christian and Celtic traditions. All that need be noted here is that the catholic Christian commitment to seeing creation as good in its origins, essence, and material existence is expressed in the mythic memory of primal unmitigated natural goodness, yet the sense of some profoundly distorting catastrophe tied to the malicious activities of beings of greater power and intelligence than ourselves, but in which we also are caught up, expresses the existential sense of tragedy and the immediately known need for redemption in the fabric of our experience of creation. That is the fall. The *Christus Victor* narrative of the redemptive intervention of Christ in his incarnation, death, and resurrection, makes no sense outside of its situation within a cosmological framework of a primal Edenic natural goodness followed by a fall into a new cosmic stasis, where alienation between creatures, within humanity, and between God and humanity is expressed in violence and death. Saint Paul's reflections on the travail of creation, of our all being dead in Adam and in slavery to sin, and of our participation in the death-overcoming life of the resurrected Christ is no side thought to the Christian faith. The salvation narrative of Christianity is that Christ overcomes the enemies of humanity (death, sickness, the maliciously daemonic, and sin) and recovers the distorted (but not destroyed) primal goodness of creation, but in a way that is not simply in time. The Pascal mystery is essentially situated "before the foundation of the world," *and* in the specificity of space-time at Jerusalem circa 33 AD, *and* partially in the kingdom of God expressed in the church age, *and* fully in the eschatological realization of redemption when both creation and all the nations are finally healed.

We cannot actually live as if pointless suffering is the final ontic reality in which we have been unwillingly thrust, for the Edenic memory and the eschatological hope are expressed in the very will to live of even the most brutal. We are brutal and destructive either for some supposed higher good (American freedom, the Communist Revolution, the Jihad against the enemies of God), out of a desire to dominate others so that we ourselves might live and thrive (self-love turned pathological), or out of inner anger caused by the violent revolt against the apparent barbarity and meaningless of reality—we do not simply take life and cause suffering with indifferent or happily satisfied workmanship. We recognize that a lack of human empathy and the absence of good will toward others as a general disposition is a profound psychological and spiritual dysfunction. Of course, technological and organizational interfaces that distance the perpetrator of dominating suffering from the human reality of what they are doing impersonalizes and pragmatizes evil, with great efficiency gains in killing and destroying as a result. Thus, Hannah Arendt can find Eichmann to hide his evil from himself in the banality of being a good bureaucrat. Peter W. Singer can note the astonishing speed with which US military strategists have rolled out and implement drones as their preferred tool of warfare because drones are staggeringly effective weapons precisely due to the manner in which they impersonalize killing by removing any physical contact with the victim and removing any physical risk to the actual killer.[17] But as natural as this all is, and as instrumentally rational as it is to use ideology, religion, technology, and bureaucracy to make "advances" in violent power, it is all profoundly pathological and a horrifying inversion of what we all actually know to be the moral fabric of the universe—goodness.

Augustine well saw that where our first love is not directed toward God, who is that goodness beyond being that Plato contemplated, then all the pathologies of human evil arise. Even so, these pathologies are not positive realities in their own right, and even so, the modus of personal glory is love directed toward the wrong final end. The ability to do evil is a function of pathologies of self-love, of which hatred is the most obviously pathological. One must be spiritually damaged in order to do damage to others or oneself, and this damage is done in the arena of the relation of the self to love.

Love is a basic existential reality in personal identity and in moral engagement with the world. It is also simply there undergirding reality. To

---

17. Arendt, *Eichmann in Jerusalem*; Singer, *Wired for War*.

not take the reality of love as of primary significance when our actions are guided by so-called pragmatic and so-called realistic instrumentalism is to ignore the reality in which we actually live and to embed our actions in abstractions and morally delusional fictions.

The Uncontainable In-Breaking of the Noumenal

The great German philosopher Immanuel Kant premised his work on the unknowability of the real. To Kant, we do not know the noumenal—things in themselves. Because we only know phenomena (the way reality *appears* to us within our own consciousness) a knowledge of the structure and workings of our consciousness replaces a knowledge of reality for Kant. The beauty of Kant's thought is that by this rigid metaphysical limitation he aims to overcome both the abstract truth-knowing "over-reach" of eighteenth-century rationalism and the concrete truth-knowing "under-reach" of eighteenth-century empiricism. In effect, Kant's powerful thought endeavored to make metaphysics redundant in both rationalist and empiricist directions. Even though the high idealist philosophy of Hegel was immediately posited against the Kantian reduction of the reality of being to the categories of phenomenal knowing, Kant's anti-metaphysical trajectory has remained with us in modern Western thinking. Kant here shows us where Descartes' move seeking to ground truth in the knowledge of the atomic thinking subject takes us. However persuasive or unpersuasive Kant's trajectory may be philosophically, it is not believable existentially.[18]

The relation of phenomena (how things appear to my thinking experience) to noumena (how things really are, independent of how I experience them) is certainly no easy nut to crack, as the history of Western philosophy from its origins in the pre-Socratics illustrates. However, the difficulty of this problem can be dishonestly negated by attempting to show that it is not a problem at all. Here we can seek to show that phenomena has an immediate and fully correlated relation to noumena, or that phenomena functionally is noumena. That is, we can *equate* our experience of reality with reality itself or we can *reduce* reality itself to our experience of reality. Rejecting both of these options, Plato advocated that we must live with the

---

18. Kant is certainly one of the modern Western greats, yet there are good reasons to find his work not only problematic in its own terms, but premised on grounds that simply cannot be justified. See Johann Georg Hamann, "Metacritique on the Purism of Reason," in Haynes (ed.) *Hamann: Writings on Philosophy and Language*, 205–18.

tension of not being able to "solve" the problem of gaining conceptual or epistemic mastery over the relation between phenomena and noumena.

To take Plato's trajectory one has to show good faith in our *partial* knowledge of how existing things really are. This good faith cannot be reduced to certain knowledge within the parameters of human comprehension, either by equating reality with our experience of immediate and "pure" material immanence, or by the abstracting the real into a realm of "pure" abstract thought. Thus, the ontology, the real being of things, is *partially* known by us—because our own being is also embedded in reality—rather than the knowing soul having a *complete* knowledge of either pure phenomena or pure noumena.

Thinking along Plato's lines it must be pointed out that I cannot prove to you that we do have a partial knowledge of the true nature and meaning of reality. The reason no proof can be given to support this stance is that showing good faith regarding a partial understanding and knowledge of the real is the most primitive premise of meaningful knowledge and valid thought, and a premise that we simply existentially know to be true. Any thinking and knowledge that does not presuppose this does not take thinking and knowing seriously, does not suppose a meaningful and knowable (yet un-masterable) reality. Further, to exploit the partial nature of our knowledge of the facts and meanings of reality in such a manner as to negate *any* real contact with reality, or to abnegate the truth-seeking nature of all human thought by being merely interested in manipulative power ("sophism" in Plato's lectionary) cannot be seen as an innocent mistake. There is a moral aspect to knowledge and meaning such that the spinning of illusions, the fostering of delusions, the rigid adherence to abstractions and known constructions because they offer manipulative power or are embedded in structures of power, is never innocent.

On things that actually concern us, things that confront us in the context of our real existence, we *do* know something of the truth about reality. We do not know everything, and we do not even know what knowledge itself is, but we also do not know nothing. We always bring something to our understanding of the real that is contingently immanently situated, but this does not reduce our knowledge of the real to mere contingency. In the post-Kantian world in which we live, a skepticism concerning any true knowledge of reality has coincided with an interest in pragmatic manipulative potency such that what one can *do* is now the functional realm of "truth" and any "beliefs" about the real intrinsic meaning or nature of anything is relegated to the subjective realm of contingently framed, entirely relative and instrumentally motivated, hermeneutic constructions. This is a world that thrives on the solipsistic satisfactions of virtuality—in entertainment, money, and market-situated identity construction—as well as being fabulously, instrumentally manipulative of impressions and desires for purposes concerned with merely practical goals; such as wealth generation, political persuasion, herd control, and status advancement. But it is all false. We do, to some extent, know the truth about reality, and one of those things that we know is that mere manipulative instrumentality is sub-human.

We have developed an "adult," "objective," and common way of life that abstractly and intellectually blanks out the moral implications of our actions. We see this as a mature and worldly-wise realism. Indeed, we achieve an "adult" outlook by rejecting what every mother teaches her child about right and wrong, and coming to think that an entirely pragmatic conception of instrumental power is simply how things are. We have produced a "realism" that is entirely blind to the *realities* of value and meaning and is only able to see what is technologically and legally doable. Even so, we do not really believe this "realism" because we actually know that meaning and value are basic to our existence. So we are actually—if tacitly—*deciding* to go with the existentially impossible when we locate power with an amoral, "purely" immanent arena of public action which is only constrained by the conventions of various governing organizations. So where legally proscribed actions put limits on the ability to do something that is both technologically possible and pragmatically advantageous to the organization that wants to do it, if the culture within the organization is governed by a tacit anti-metaphysics of instrumental realism, the organization will not simply accept the legal constraints on its own pursuit of pragmatic advantage, but will get busy with lawyers and the courts and find a way to do what it wants to do anyway. Indeed, governments do this too, where the "national interest" is at stake. My own government—Australia—spied on sensitive negotiations with the East Timorese about who has the rightful ownership of oil in the Timor Sea. Timor is one of the poorest nations on earth and Australia is—by global standards—a very rich nation. The Australian government successfully used its internal knowledge of the negotiating process to gain stunningly unfair access for Australian-based corporate interests to the only natural resource this poor country has. This was considered to be a valid enterprise in realpolitik espionage and a canny negotiation manipulation that was justified because it advanced the "national interest" of the Australian state.[19] Spy networks that treat the laws of other nations and the privacy rights of its own citizens as no obstacle to advancing or protecting the "national interest" rely on a farcical amoralism shrouded in official secrecy that presupposes what we all know is false; that manipulative competitive advantage is justified by any means that succeeds. And, alas, it cannot be denied that in fabulously lucrative and geopolitically sensitive arenas—such as illegal international arms trading—the dynamics portrayed in the movie *Lord of War* are not fictitious.[20] Here global military empires—and there are none bigger than the USA—foster covert ties with powerful criminal cartels to support the industries of violence, terror, and exploitation such that this brute amoral potency can be used to their own advantage when needs be. At a less overtly violent level, but within an equally pragmatic and power-centric mindset, the logic of high finance can escape human and economic reality via complex financial instruments.[21] Here derivative trading can bring down real economies—as we saw in the 2008 crisis—with devastating consequences for real people's lives, leaving many regions of the global economy in crisis.[22] Yet no-one responsible for these fiscal meltdowns, no-one responsible for astronomical transfer of government money into private banking hands, goes to jail.[23] Equally, the manner in which the financial crisis in the Eurozone was played out in 2015 made it abundantly clear that the political determinations of Greece were of no concern to the centers of European and global fiscal power. This shows the tendency of instrumental high power to ignore what we actually know about our moral responsibilities to each other, so that we can maintain our control over the tools of power at any cost. This is only possible because we have lost track of the fact that we *do* know what we *should* do, and that no excuse grounded in a "realist" amoral account of what we pragmatically *must* do has any grounding in truth. We seem to let the powerful believe that we also do not know what the moral meaning of the actions of self-serving subhuman power *really* is. But we do know.

19. See Cannane, Koloff, and Andersen, "'Matter of Death and Life': Espionage in East Timor and Australia's Diplomatic Bungle."

20. Niccol, *Lord of War*. Amnesty International strongly endorses this movie, http://www.amnestyusa.org/pdfs/lordofwar_edguide.pdf.

21. Das, *Traders, Guns and Money*; Das, *Extreme Money*.

22. Varoufakis, *The Global Minotaur*; Varoufakis, *And the Weak Suffer What They Must?*

23. Ferguson, *Inside Job*; Taibbi, *Griftopia*; Lewis, *The Big Short*.

The manner in which the noumenal is outlawed from the realm of knowledge has significantly shaped the very nature of the university after Kant. For now, it is reflexive for our most intelligent thinkers in the humanities and social sciences to give precedent to fictitious constructs we know are not true over substantive meanings that we know are, at the very least, important.

There are a host of books on the market in what might be called the disaffected academic genre. Richard Hil's *Whackademia* is just one of them. As stated on the back cover, Hil's book "lifts the lid on a higher education system that is corporatized beyond recognition, steeped in bureaucracy and dominated by marketing and PR imperatives rather than intellectual pursuits." The trend in the demise of the very idea that universities exist in order to pursue substantively valuable goals—like humanizing its students and the pursuit of truth—is driven by the manner in which pragmatic instrumental "realism" has embedded itself in the administrative apparatus of the modern university. Of course, this "realism" is an entirely existentially unrealistic commitment to the "value" of administratively constructed academic metrics (that are used to facilitate institutional financial cost/benefit calculations) and the operational norms of today's corporate commercial culture. But this trend is not merely an institutional imposition on scholars. Scholarship itself has a long tradition of existential vacuity which was profoundly assisted by the anti-metaphysical turn of the late Enlightenment. Actually, there are two traditions in scholarship in the West, both of which have their roots in antiquity: a sophistic academic tradition and a tradition where thought about truth is both possible and really matters.

Again, we know that thought really matters, but modern scholarship lends itself in a distinctively sophisticated manner to its own internal world of accepted processes, assumed (but entirely constructed) orthodoxies, and conformity to the norms of recognition and status as defined by established elites and their "in"-peers. Such sophism need have no reference to anything outside of the highly politically and egotistically charged workings of professional academia. Hence, arcane armchair "scholasticism" has never been more virulent in our universities than it is today. A significant reason for this is a broad tacit acceptance in academia of a Kantian anti-metaphysical skepticism such that "knowledge production" could not be anything other than a game for smart people where process, conformity to scholarly consensus, peer recognition, and funding grants are the only "truths" than finally matters. Mavericks who challenge any established interpretive orthodoxy as if it was *wrong*, and as if an alternative was potentially *right*, and as if right or wrong thinking about truth *actually mattered* in the world today, are not happily tolerated within the academy. No, solid, "non-polemic" scholarship is an endless armchair argument about sources and interpretations and one has to have astonishingly specialized and arcane knowledge to participate in this intricate dance of minds with any grace. But in the end, it is an aesthetic contest. Essentially, the point of such scholarship is to display one's scholarly prowess, rather than to uncover any substantive truth that actually matters for today. For it is "safe" as a scholar to write *about* the arguments of real philosophers, and it is good team form for a scholar to construct an intricate source-based assault on the details of scholarship done by some maverick outsider who dares try to advance truth against any well-accepted scholarly consensus, but only rarely will you find a scholar with enough heat in their belly to actually reason about their field as if the truth really matters, for here, for now. We have divorced existential passion from scholarly activity because the scholar's enterprise is tacitly understood to have no real contact with reality.

How We Came to Believe What We Know Isn't True, and to Disbelieve What We Know Is True

Our life-world is the set of common operational value-, meaning-, and power-assumptions in which we live. This set defines the shared norms and reality-assumptions underpinning the very structures of how we work, love, trade, succeed, fail, play, relate socially, find significance, and think of ourselves and the world. Within the life-world of Western modernity our understanding of being, knowing, and believing is largely passive. Here being is unknowable, knowing is objectified and qualitatively meaningless, and believing is atomistically subjectified and its meanings and commitments are receptively constructed. This passivity, and this distinctive type of unknowing, objectivity, and subjectivity, makes our life-world's arena of public action—"the real world"™—strikingly divorced from the existential realities we know to be true. How did we come to live like this?

The conceptual genealogy of our present life-form is very interesting and is a very long and intricate story. I will not directly explore that here, though I think John Milbank's *Theology and Social Theory* opens up a very useful vista in seeking to uncover the roots of the modern life-world in a range of medieval theological developments.[24] Sidestepping the interminable intricacies of genealogical scholastic debate, however, I wish to explore the question of how we got to where we are in more concrete terms. Starting with the here and now, it is clear that our life-world privileges objective instrumental power and subjectivized self-construction over existential reality. In functional terms, the way our life-world works is deeply shaped by the history of finance in the twentieth century.

There are two globally significant financial events in the twentieth century that have shaped our life-world. These events both happened in the USA, which is the dominant power-player of the post-war global order in which we now live. I refer to the Wall Street crash of 1929 and the abandonment of the gold standard by the Nixon administration in 1971.

The Great Depression of the 1930s saw the demise of the last form of the yeoman farmer and rural village life in the USA. At the same time that there were horrifying artificially induced famines in the USSR, millions of rural Americans also perished in the combined hardships of drought, bankruptcy, and alienation from their rural way of life. The way of life where most of the common people were primary food producers living on the land died in the USA in the 1930s. It was killed off by financial hardship so that small family farms were bought up for a song by large conglomerates, and where—after the war—heavy machinery made most farm labor redundant. The common people then became urban dwellers and wage earners, and useful for the rich entrepreneurs as factory workers and consumers. The manner in which localized rural life—with its churches, its political structures, its close-knit communities, its need of rural labor, and its connections to the rhythms and limits of nature—was made redundant and replaced by large impersonal urban contexts cannot be over-emphasized as a transformer of the life-world norms of US life, the flagship of modern consumer society. In response to the Great Depression the New Deal sought to bring relief, recovery and reform, but the boom years of the American economy did not get going until the 1940s. World War Two provided work and the impetus for massive public spending on war-related industry, and this saw the US recover from its economic hardships as well as ushering in the "Green Revolution," where heavy farming machinery and large farming conglomerates replaced the small family farm and the rural workforce.

The new world order that emerged out of the carnage of the Second World War was dominated by US manufacturing, financial, military,

24. Milbank, *Theology and Social Theory.*

ideological, and cultural power from the start. The dynamism of the US-led post-war reconstruction was astonishing, and it was an era of optimism and prosperity for those national powers around the world, either defeated and rebuilt by the Allies (with the US funding the re-construction of German and Japan in particular) or directly linked in with the "free world" capitalist ideology of the American-led victors. Cheap oil, low inflation, high employment, governments committed to large public works programs, sustained growth, and confidence and opportunity at every turn characterized the most economically constructive era of the twentieth century for Western nations—the post-war boom. Yet, the narrative of freedom and opportunity for all was challenged by the USSR. This challenge was not left unanswered, and thus came the Cold War. It was the Cold War that brought the post-war boom of 1949–71 to an end. This is because the Space Race, the Korean War, and the Vietnam War proved so astronomically expensive for the USA that even the dynamism and size of its originally buoyant surplus economy was transformed into a deficit economy by the late 1960s. When the Nixon Administration dropped the gold standard—a mechanism for preventing currency trading and for carefully limiting the type of speculative financial escape from the real economy characteristic of the roaring 20s—this signaled the end of the post-war era and the collapse of a key feature of the Bretton Woods architecture underpinning the (non-communist) global economy. The result was that "the free world" of the 1970s saw stagflation—rising inflation and rising unemployment—as the American-centric global capitalist world order was re-configured around the US deficit economy and Wall Street and London were unleashed from the constraints of a financial environment tied in some manner to the real economy.

In the post-1971 period to the present, some distinctive features of global economics and national politics became apparent. Nations tied to the US-led post-war era gave up the goal of having control over their own economies and followed the US in tying themselves to the concept of competitive advantage in "the global economy." The idea here was that Third World countries had the "competitive advantage" of being rich in cheap unskilled labor and natural resources whereas First World countries had high technology knowledge and expertise and were rich in money and financial knowhow. So, particularly from the 1980s, many tariff barriers protecting national industries were pulled down, many national assets were sold off to powerful private investors, financial institutions increasingly engaged in speculative trading, and multi-national corporations became increasingly unaccountable to national political governance.[25] The disappearance of the USSR in the late 1980s removed any serious ideological challenge to the US-led global world order, with changes in the Chinese Communist Party making it possible for China to play (and increasingly win) a modified version of the game of competitive advantage as given them by the US. And, of course, there can be no doubt that the exploitation of cheap labor and resources in the global south by financially powerful "private" forces in the global north has proved to deliver continuous profits to the existing corporate powers who now treat the globe as their property, increasingly free from the constraints of national political governance. The relationship between powerful corporations and national governments is increasingly one where the state is guarantor and supporter of private corporate profits in exchange for the benefits of economic growth, which are supposed to signal wealth and prosperity in the civic populace. But whatever the rights and wrongs and financial costs and benefits of this situation may be, the point of significance here is what this context does in relation to defining the life-world "realities" in which we all live now.

It is apparent that the life-world we now inhabit is radically disconnected from the moral and physical realities of our existence, which were more locally and religiously integral with our mode of life before the astonishing political, employment, financial, and urbanized transformations of Western life effected in the twentieth century. Political power is now more or less a derivative feature of financial power, financial power is now largely disconnected from moral and religious constraint, and an instrumental pragmatism is the ruling practice of "realism" native to the world in which we live. By the early decades of the twenty-first century the global north (the power center of the new increasingly post-political global capitalist civilization) has more or less lost living contact with the catastrophic dysfunction of the Great Depression and the horrors, devastation, and destruction of modern war. That we are replicating the conditions for both does not seem to have any traction on our polities, which are now largely cosmetic appendages to global financial and geopolitical military power. After the demise of communism as an ideology, which might be a global alternative to the present world order, the new threat to global good order—Islamic terrorism—is neatly seen as an external threat. In fact, violent religious extremism is directly thrown up by the moral and

25. Ferguson, *Inside Job*, 24–52.

religious disconnect from reality characteristic of our life-world and the systemic global exploitation that life-world relies on for its perpetuation. This is a stress fracture arising from *within* our life-world, affording us a dire warning should power continue to function as it does. The stresses on the Eurozone and the unresponsiveness of Europe's fiscal masters to the political necessities of economically bankrupt states is another stress fracture. The environmental degradation of China is another stress fracture. There are many signs that our life-world cannot continue in its present form for much longer without radical change. But we are fairly locked into it by the very way we in the global north now typically live; an urban wage-earning life as consumers of goods, services, and entertainments provided by the global powers that we now simply serve.

In this context, alternative ways of living—ways that maintain a connection to the religious and moral realities of our existence—are more or less divorced from the governing powers under which we live.

Life-world and Being, Knowing, and Believing

There is a close tie-in between the mass media, the financial, the civic-political, and the geopolitical structures of the operational norms of the life-world of consumer society and the dominant assumptions of our distinctive way of understanding knowledge and belief, and of not understanding being. There is nothing inherently fundamental about the way we think of knowing and believing, and hence the way we don't think about being, but that way of thinking is integral with the structures of our life-world, and is tied in with the curious dislocation between existential realities and the "objective" world of power and action in which we live. But the (socially constructed) reality is that the very idea of being makes no sense to our life-world. Let us now further explore why this situation is inherently bad in an endeavor to recover the importance of being in our times.

4

THE FORGETFULNESS OF BEING IS
AN INHERENTLY BAD THING

Readers with some sense of familiarity with the work of John Milbank will recognize important areas of continuity between this little book and Milbank's thesis. The nub of Milbank's argument is that modern secular reason, and its liberal, market-orientated, consumerist life-form, is histori-cally caused by a family of developments in late medieval Western theology. To put it in un-nuanced terms, Milbank argues that these developments are both theologically defective and have an increasingly negative impact on Western culture the more entrenched they become.

Milbank is not the only thinker to argue that a tacitly theological sub-structure underpins modern Western secularism and shapes the specific political, economic, cultural, and intellectual topography of our way of life. Indeed, the rejection of a progressive and Enlightenment account of Western secular modernity has strong nineteenth-century antecedents from think-ers as diverse as Nietzsche and Kierkegaard. In our times, the American an-thropologist Talal Asad also finds that contemporary Western secularism is no less laden with unprovable premises and destructive tendencies than any other way of life.[1] Sociologists are also often familiar with the degree to which liberal Western secularism is a complex culturo-political construct,

---

1. Asad, *Formations of the Secular.*

rather than the apex of political freedom and hard-headed reasoning that those within its life-form typically assume it to be.

Milbank's work is controversial. If you take the time and considerable effort required to follow the scholarly arguments which supporters and detractors of Milbank's work engage in, two things become apparent. Firstly, arguments about the accurate interpretation of great thinkers from the past—particularly Thomas Aquinas and Duns Scotus—are interminable arenas of arcane one-upmanship. Secondly, those who claim Milbank's reading of Aquinas and Scotus is tendentious often actively dislike what they see as Milbank's nostalgic glamorization of pre-Scotist Neoplatonist theology and philosophy. Tracing the dysfunctions of modernity to fourteenth-century theological errors is seen as imposing a narrative of decline on the way Milbank interprets the history of modernity. There are two possible reasons for this. One is a rigid commitment to an academic methodology that (ironically) maintains that a non-appraisal of the qualitative direction of any genealogical development is *good* scholarship, the other is a tacit acceptance of the modern Western narrative of progress.

In this little book I am arguing that our loss of the ontological heritage of Western thinking—which is now so entrenched as to entail the loss of the very language of truth categories via which we can appreciate the mystery of being—is a real loss which has destructive implications for the conditions of human (and non-human) life within our contemporary life-world. This is not a nostalgic narrative of decline, vainly hankering after the return of the now lost life-world of medieval Christendom, it is a nuanced narrative of a particular loss and of forward-looking reconstructive advocacy. I wish to argue that while it is obviously the case that we did lose a distinctive form of approaching the truth of being, more than that, we also lost the very idea of the truth of being, and this is a true loss. In light of this loss, I will argue that we need to recover a metaphysically viable understanding of the truth and meaning of being, and we need to develop a new (that is, contingent, contextual, and imaginative) reconstruction of our way of life in light of that recovery. But there are two alternative stances to what I am here advocating. Firstly, there is the stance that maintains that history does not have a qualitative direction, for developments do not get better or worse, they just develop. Secondly, there is the stance which maintains that the very things I am decrying—forgetfulness of being, pragmatic instrumental conceptions of knowledge and power, the subjectification of belief—are actually good and genuinely progressive developments. In this chapter I will examine the two alternative understandings of forgetfulness of being in order to disclose them as misguided, and I will then explore why forgetfulness of being is a genuine loss and how that loss shapes our life-world destructively.

Is the Forgetfulness of Being a Value-Neutral "Mere Development" in Western Culture?

The idea that things just develop, without getting in some ways better, in other ways worse, or the idea that all qualitative judgments are entirely relative to the interests of those who make those judgments, is the rejection of credence toward the ontological reality of value itself. Or, which has the same effect, it is the rejection of the knowability of real value. That is, qualitative agnosticism is a function of a distinctive type of ontological skepticism. Until the modern Western era, qualitative agnosticism was not taken seriously in terms of how people actually lived, as people were—in general—not ontological skeptics. Religion—as a creative cultural tie-in between our collectively situated mundane way of life and the partially manifest qualitative and transcendent realities in which the cosmos is grounded—is naturally integral with politics, trade, law, morality, and learning in every culture bar our own. So the modern Western secular assumption that any cultural development is a "mere development," and not a development that is qualitatively assessable, is symptomatic of Western modernity's ontological skepticism. It is not (ironically) a value-neutral and assumption-free commitment to "mere" objectivity.

There are a range of practices deeply embedded in the life-world of modern Western secular culture that maintain the operational fiction of value-neutral, rationally necessary, interpretively simple, pragmatically self-authenticating, objective knowledge. The discourse of scientific knowledge has displaced the very idea of ontological knowledge and presupposes that the non-material beings and meanings of religion have no real relation to reality. More precisely, the rise of scientific knowledge is tied to the rejection of the late medieval edifice of ontological knowledge tied in with religion, but then once science had replaced the medieval approach to ontology, it was unable to produce a viable ontology of its own, but sought to define ontology in terms of value-neutral, objectively quantifiable, mathematically speculative "metaphysics" (which is actually, just physics, but not done by real physicists). This had the effect of defining ontology into non-existence.

However, the modern enterprise to use science as the sole measure of truth was always philosophically tenuous, and came unstuck badly during the course of modern philosophy. Modern Western philosophy now suffers from a collapse of confidence in the epistemological foundationalism that gave it birth, as illustrated, for example, by the intractable conundrums of logical positivism and the rise of the postmodern critique of the metanarrative of scientific objectivity. Those determined to continue the modern Western approach to philosophy tend to be Anglo-American analytical and empirical reductionists who simply ignore "Continental" thought. Thus, modern Anglo-American metaphysics has become an increasingly arcane field of mathematical and scientific speculation disconnected from the increasingly postmodern cultural sensibilities of consumer society. Ironically, the cultural embracing of virtuality and the pragmatic abandonment of truth, which is increasingly the hallmark of our hypermodern life-world, is a natural corollary of the evacuation of meaning and value from ontology native to the idea of the modern fact. But this is also out of touch with larger developments in Western hermeneutic philosophy, the sociology of knowledge, and the philosophy of science.

Since Nietzsche, Kuhn, Polanyi, Berger, Ricoeur, Foucault, etc., a much more nuanced understanding of the cultural, political, and interpretive context of all knowledge constructions has informed our appreciation of how functionally impossible it is to get to any purely rational or purely empirical foundation for knowledge (the holy grail of modern philosophy). We now appreciate that meaningful and communally situated interpretive contexts embedded in existing culturally assumed narratives, existing structures of norms, power, and practices, are functionally prior to knowledge. That is, we now know that there is no more basic epistemological foundation than practice informing myth. In other words, meaning received from the basic narratives one simply inherits from one's culture is prior to the knowledge constructs produced by the recognized truth-telling authorities embedded in that culture. This is just as true in ancient Bronze Age Athens as it is in modern scientific California.

In the context of modernity, the idea of value-neutral objective knowledge is a useful but unavoidably poetic construct. Most importantly, the impartial "mere" facticity of modern knowledge is a powerful fiction that is integral with modern power. As integral with power, the epistemic pragmatism of modernity ensures that an appreciation of the fictive nature of modern truth does not entail functional disbelief in that fiction. Explicitly, this value-neutral fiction is (ironically) deemed valuable in modernity, such that naïve positivism, naïve rationalism, naïve materialistic reductionism, and a naïve narrative of objective scientific truth is the methodological underpinning of scholarly credibility. So while, after Ricoeur, Foucault, etc., few serious scholars within the humanities and social sciences would *say* they believe the fiction of mere facticity in modern knowledge—and many genuinely know that this is a fiction—they do actually (and actively) believe this fiction, and must if they are to be taken seriously as experts of modern knowledge.

In the scholarly arena, the reductive and instrumental positivistic rationality of modernity is a rationality scholars have high levels of expertise in, know how to manipulate, and are familiar with. Further, it is in fact vital that people operationally believe in modern truth in order to maintain the modern secular technological and liberal life-world in which we actually live. The scholar performs a priest function in legitimating the prevailing norms under which power and meaning are constructed for us as true.

So let us take the fiction of non-qualitative, hermeneutically simple cultural analysis seriously—that is, let us take this myth as a serious sociopolitical construct necessary for the operation of our way of life—and explore its strengths and weaknesses.

Exploring the Modern Belief in the Truth of Science

The dominant account of the origins of modern knowledge are tied up with the clash between Galileo's empirically and mathematically supported heliocentric cosmology and the medieval geocentric cosmology derived from Aristotelian natural philosophy combined with the dogmatic theology endorsed by the Roman Catholic church and established university learning. It should not be thought that empirical observation and careful mathematical modelling were foreign to the geocentric model that Newton finally completely displaced. But when one reads Francis Bacon and the early documents of the Royal Society of London for Improving Natural Knowledge, it is clear that the new natural learning was notable for being *only* interested in the advances and uses of "physico-mathematical experimental learning." That is, what separates modern scientific truth from the natural philosophy and dogmatic theology of the late medieval university is not the use of mathematical modelling and careful observation, but the preparedness to rely *exclusively* on such knowledge to the exclusion of metaphysics, moral philosophy, theological knowledge, and doctrinal fealty. Modern knowledge is artificially reductive, instrumentally authenticating, and metaphysically and hermeneutically naïve in its very nature. And, of course, what is so attractive about this form of knowledge is how astonishingly instrumentally useful it is. But that is not all. It was also understood by its seventeenth-century advocates as true in direct contrast to false metaphysically, theologically, and dogmatically framed knowledge.

Newton's celestial mechanics decisively ended Aristotelian geocentric cosmology by the combination of mathematical proofs of natural laws grounded in immediate observation and used to form accurate predictions. This method's triumph over knowledge grounded in ancient and church authority signaled a new age of freedom from authority, and this freedom was understood as liberation from falsehood. Modern knowledge is embedded in a narrative of a scientific and mathematical liberation from falsehood delivering to us a new and true age of reason and power, accompanied by a bold and decisive rejection of all things medieval. To the Enlightenment vision of the eighteenth century, what we now call "medieval" was synonymous with false speculative metaphysics, superstition, ineffectual magic, and blind loyalty to irrational authority.

Question This Narrative of the Birth of Modern Truth

If the evidence of the senses and a rational understanding of natural mechanics are to be *believed*, then clearly the heliocentric cosmology is true and the geocentric cosmology is false. Indeed, what could be more reasonable than *believing* that sense and logic divulge truth to us? The point to note here is that the medievals were just as dedicated to believing sensation and logic as truth mediums as were the early moderns. Trust in the truth of logic and the senses is not what separates the medievals from the early moderns, which is why a heliocentric cosmology was able to replace, as true, the medieval geocentric cosmology (though not without a very slow inertial swing away from the established interpretive paradigm, as Kuhn well describes).[2] Indeed, entirely medieval thinking had much to do with Copernicus' initial proposition of heliocentrism. The influence of Platonism on Renaissance Italy, and the metaphysical significance of the sun as a natural analogy for the goodness-beyond-being, and of God Himself, figures as a significant background influence on Copernicus' mathematical

---

2. Kuhn, *Structure of Scientific Revolutions*.

attempt to overcome the staggering complexity of Aristotelian calculations of planetary motion. So the medieval and early modern propensity to *believe* sense and logic as truth-revealing gives them more in common with each other than either of them have with a postmodern disbelief in all metanarratives of objective truth. Indeed, Royal Society types in the mold of Francis Bacon really did *believe* that observation and reason gave us truth. This credibility trajectory should be differentiated from another trajectory also basic to modernity, which is the skeptical trajectory seen in the influence of Sextus Empiricus on the likes of Descartes and Hume. Descartes (contra Empiricus) and Kant (contra Hume) endeavor to establish indubitable truth-criteria in response to the powerful impetus to *not* believe sense or reason as truth-revealing. But since the nineteenth century it has been clear that modern arguments against not believing have failed. And it is the failure of the attempt to overcome modern skepticism —the attempt to give us indubitable proof grounded in pure sense and pure logic—that locates the postmodern suspicion of the very idea of truth as grounded in both of the major intellectual trajectories of modernity.

Practically, one naturally believes the normal veracity of the senses and reason. But this is believing as an *active and public* response to the vision of reality that sense and reason reveal. This is not "believing" in the modern sense of internalized interpretive glosses that are not subject to scientific proof and that reflect the private freedoms of conscience to hold whatever religious and moral convictions (or none) that one wishes. Rather, believing as an active and public process is always tied in with the culturally situated interpretive norms that make sense of sensation and that define the parameters of true and false reasoning. All of our actual ways of understanding the (at least partially) true meaning of sense and reason require a degree of *trust* in the ever-hermeneutically-mediated grounds of sense and reason as truth-revealing. Modernity, however, wished to replace belief with *proof* and mediation with *self-evident immediacy*. But then finding proof of the veracity of meanings delivered to us by sense and reason in a manner that did not appeal to any sort of belief and that was not circular (ironically) proved to be impossible. Seeking to isolate veracity in terms of empirical and rational proof had the effect of subjectivizing belief and entrenching a fundamental suspicion of all objective and public forms of belief. It is no surprise, then, that mere pragmatism and virtuality have now functionally replaced the credibility mentality of Enlightenment-styled confidence in a scientific age of reason within contemporary Western culture. Now our high culture is incoherently committed to both fundamental qualitative relativism and the theatre of objective knowledge which has in fact replaced meaningful truth with power.

A central feature of this astonishingly unsatisfactory situation is that the (impossible) narrative of objective factual truth being entirely discrete from subjective fictions about meaning and value undermines the credibility of our senses and reason and yet still heartily finds religion and understandings of moral reality to be inadmissible as knowledge because they cannot be proved by sense or reason. This is our discourse of knowledge. And while both modern and postmodern approaches to truth deny that there could be real and partially knowable ontological and qualitative truth that we might reasonably believe, at least postmodern understandings are more consistent as a system of belief-suspicion than modern scientism.

The idea that there really is no objective qualitative meaning to historical developments is a function of the impossible modern isolation of indemonstrable belief from provable knowledge and the relegation of meaning and value to a subjective realm of (actively and publicly unbelievable) mere belief. If one is going to believe things for logically coherent reasons, this stance is too incoherent in its own terms to be taken seriously. Either one dismisses the reality of meaningful and qualitative truth entirely—and then one cannot distinguish between the truth or error of or in science, religion, magic, and fiction (though one may make distinctions in relation to instrumental effectiveness)—or one returns to the credibility of active and public belief as a partial truth-medium. If one dismisses the reality of meaning entirely, then this undermines the meaning of *everything* one says. This, as Plato saw, is sophistry that does not taking language, meaning, and our actual experiences seriously. If one wants to hold to the believability of science as truth, then one has to revive the idea of the truth-revealing function of belief. If one does that, the narrative of modernity—of the replacement of belief with proof—needs to be dropped.

For the above reasons I will not take the idea that there is no true meaning or qualitative direction to historical developments as being a serious stance that even could be true. Thus, the question of whether the loss of the very idea of ontological truth from Western culture is a good development or a bad development should be taken seriously. Let us take a critical look at the argument that this loss was a good development.

Is the Narrative of Progress Integral with an Enlightenment Understanding of the Modern Era Valid?

The modern life-world is grounded in a deeply believed cosmogenic narrative that maintains that the separation of empirical and rational proof from religiously and metaphysically grounded (active and public) beliefs is a genuine truth-revealing and liberty-promoting improvement on the medieval life-world. This is progress. Then the staggering advances in scientific knowledge and technological power which modernity has seen is evidence of the superiority of modernity over the medieval world. Who would want to return to life without penicillin, jet travel, modern medicine, and the modern mass production of high technology consumer goods? Who would want to return to a society where there were inquisitions, autocratic power, the burning of witches, and the killing of heretics? Clearly, we have progressed. That the modern world is defined by advances in a true understanding of nature, advances in power over nature, and advances in the rational governance of society are all tacit assumptions basic to the modern life-world. Yet clearly, this progress is integral with what could well be called modernity's forgetfulness of being.

If one believes in the partial truth-revealing capacities of sense and reason—as I do—then it is very clear that modern scientific knowledge illustrates staggering advances toward a better understanding of factual truth in many areas, compared to the knowledge discourses of late medieval Aristotelian natural philosophy. It is also true that there really are progressive aspects to modernity. But the picture is complex. I wish to argue that in some directions modernity has been progressive and in other directions it has been regressive. How we understand the meaning of progressive and regressive is the matter of contention.

Progressing toward What?

To think clearly about progress we must, ironically, turn to the science of teleology. I say ironically, because the science of teleology is one area where a good argument can be made showing a staggering intellectual regress within modernity as compared with pre-modern Western thought.

It is an interesting feature of Darwinian-framed biology—at least at a popular cultural level—that this way of thinking is embedded in an understanding of natural selection where survival and the quest of life against death via projection into the future through offspring, at the expense of competitors, is considered to be the primal natural good for all life forms and the basic driver of developmental progress. That is, life forms produced by "Nature" all have the same goal—survival—and this goal gives all life forms their natural *purpose*, their guiding life *aim*, thus survival defines the proper *end* of life itself. Life forms that "succeed," according to this natural goal, "advance" as they adapt to their environment in order to become more successful survivors as a species than their competitors. Thus, mere survival as *the purpose* of all living beings is considered to be a fact of science. Teleology—reasoning about purpose, about the proper ends of the actions of living beings—is thus an integral component of a Darwinist science of life. Here a teleology of progress is defined as the natural outcome of continuous improvement in survival capacities relative to a particular environment.

But just as Darwin's progressive teleology is integral with his biology, so also, for example, Aristotle's static teleology is integral with his biology. That is, the interpretive frame defining purpose in any teleology is not the *product* of any given paradigm of science, but is the *foundation* defining that paradigm of science. This can be brought out by comparing the teleology undergirding Darwin's paradigm of biological science with the teleology undergirding Aristotle's biological science.

To Darwin, competitive advantage in survival is the engine of progress and hence the ceaseless struggle for growth and improvement produces evolutionary progress. Perhaps this concept of competitively propelled progress is best illustrated in humanity, being at the top of the evolutionary tree. For clearly humans are the most successful dominating survivalists, adapting to a huge range of environments, due to the combination of opposable thumbs and language, which produces the species-wide accumulation and extension of manipulative intelligence. Further, a "Christian" understanding of a temporal beginning and eschatological motion toward a transformative, historically situated future end is also tacitly integral with Darwin's outlook, such that time has a developmental direction where the complex and advanced always has its origins in the simple and primitive. To Aristotle, in contrast, the essential forms of different beings do not change because they reflect the eternal stasis of continuous, ever-rebalancing, intrinsically meaningful motion within the cosmos.

Space and time are eternal to Aristotle. This defines a crucial area of difference between a "progressive" understanding of natural teleology as found in nineteenth-century Western science and any sort of Aristotelian conception of natural purpose. This is worth drawing out. Aristotle could not posit a temporal beginning and end in nature, for, quite sensibly, he could see no way of starting the chain of causation within the natural relations of the world. That is, to Aristotle there would need to be some "start" outside of space, time, and causation that was not itself a function of a further causal chain if nature had a spatio-temporal beginning, but such a notion violates the very principle of causality that defines spatio-temporal nature. Further, if such a "start" were itself of a non-spatio-temporal-causal nature, then how—being radically other than nature as we know it—could it touch space and time? Even so Aristotle does not think that space and time can account for themselves, but he posits a radical First Cause that is also eternal and also—in a sense—natural. Contingent causal relations within space and time, and the integral co-dependence of matter and form, are eternal for Aristotle, and there is a non-temporal and divine First Cause which accounts for causation within eternal space and time itself. To Aristotle, this First Cause—God—is also the divine mind that accounts for form and reason in the cosmos. Because Darwin's tacit teleology and cosmology assumes that time—at least for life on earth—has a start, and nature is progressing in form, this shapes the way he reads nature. Because Aristotle's explicit teleology and cosmology rejects the notion of a temporal start to life and form in nature in order to avoid the problem of eternal regress, and the problem of radically unlike arising from like (the non-living producing life) his understanding of purpose within biology is not defined by modern progressive assumptions. Philosophically, Aristotle has thought through the cosmological and causal implications of his science of life much more seriously than has Darwin. Darwin was a creative and highly astute naturalist operating within the philosophical assumptions of nineteenth-century naturalism, but he never made any claim to being a serious philosopher. But the most interesting difference between Darwin and Aristotle concerns the telos for life. In Darwin, the telos for life is *survival*; in Aristotle, it is *flourishing*.

To Aristotle, *flourishing* in complex inter-dependent harmony with other beings is life's overarching telos, rather than adaptive competitive survival. So the need to dominate embedded in the progressive urge of improving one's competitive advantage (a distinctly nineteenth-century

English imperial/capitalist outlook) is not considered to be the telos of life itself in Aristotle. This is not to say that Aristotle is a peace-loving hippy. The virtues of Greek warrior culture were integral with his understanding of biological reality too, but even so he did not see the overarching purpose of the cosmos as survivalistic (warrior virtues were not survivalistic to him either).

Let us reason along Aristotelian lines for a moment.

Survival is an inadequate teleological category because, as *mere* survival, it has no qualitative or intellective significance. Should it happen—as is quite possible—that humanity will become so dominant on the earth, and so competitively fixated with sheer dominating instrumental power, that we end up radically damaging the fecundity of the biosphere and make our own species (and many others) extinct, then the survivors of the story of life on earth may well turn out to be microbes and insects. In what sense could that development be considered as "progressing" toward some natural good? In what sense could that development be considered the fulfillment of a meaningful natural purpose reflecting the intelligible order of the cosmos as a whole? That is, the very notion of teleology is inherently qualitative and intellective, and "progress" defined in terms of mere dominating competitive advantage as a means toward survival, is teleologically meaningless. To Aristotle survival only has meaning and purpose as a *means*; it is flourishing that is the proper *end* of life. Thus, Aristotle finds it natural and scientific to notice that for humans, not being frustrated in our capacity to make and pursue rational plans guided by meaningful purposes toward valuable ends, is basic to human flourishing. Only developments that aid *that* end are progressive.

Progress cannot be defined in merely survivalistic terms if it is to have any teleological significance, and the knowledge constructs embedded in this inadequate teleology are likely to interpret biological reality in distorted ways as a function of their inadequate teleology. Leaving to one side the question of what an evolutionary biological science might look like with a more adequate teleology, let us ask how we can understand the notion of progress in a qualitative and intellectively meaningful way.

I want to try to define progress in genuinely teleological terms. That is, not in terms of supposedly amoral instrumental superiority. There can be no doubt that if progress is a function only of superior factual knowledge and instrumental power then modernity is obviously a complete advance on the life-form it superseded. Yet clearly some of modernity's knowledge and power is used toward good ends—ends that enable complex harmonies of flourishing—and some are used toward bad ends—ends distortedly defined in terms of mere dominating power; ends ultimately destructive of flourishing. When modernity's knowledge and power is used toward bad ends, this illustrates "advances" in destructive and immoral power. That is, advances in factual knowledge that undergird advances in manipulative effectiveness and instrumental efficiency are advances of *means*, not advances in, or necessarily toward, good *ends*. Progress is about movement toward good ends, this can be facilitated by powerful means, but *there is no necessary connection between advances in powerful means and progress toward valuable ends.*

Here is the really interesting thing about trying to think teleologically within modernity: that the very discourse of valuable and meaningful ends is no longer considered a field of knowledge means that teleology itself is not taken seriously, leaving us only with efficiency gains in instrumental technologies as measures of "progress." This, I wish to argue, is a genuine loss when modernity is compared to the life-form it superseded, and to all non-modern life-forms, which are distinguishable from modernity simply by having respect for teleological rationality.

Note, I am not saying that the specific structure of teleological belief in any given non-modern culture is superior to the non-teleologically framed life-form of modernity, but I am saying that simply because they have accepted common discourses of teleological rationality and modernity does not, this illustrates a loss within modernity. Teleology can be better or worse, truer to reality or less true to reality, just like any other system of common belief. I also maintain that modernity has a *tacit* but defective teleology. We have a teleology of dominating power, freed from any constraints of rational or moral purpose, or common good, or divine fealty. But this is a degraded teleology precisely because it is supposedly merely factual, where facts are understood to have only empirical and rational content and no value, no hermeneutic meaning, and no inherent and proper end. Further, as the teleology of modernity is *only* tacit, it is highly resistive to any rational discourse of meaningful knowledge.[3]

---

3. There is a secularized version of Christian cosmological beginning and eschatological end to space and time and thus a naturalistic conception of temporal cosmic "progress," and a strange attempt to reframe moral realist assumptions in terms of amoral reality such that it is "good" to survive and dominate. These are inherently incoherent notions such that the naturalistic teleology of modernity *must* remain tacit, for it could not survive serious philosophical or theological examination if made explicit.

But let us be as charitable as possible to the modern idea of progress, and look at it in the terms of the liberal morality and democratic politics it thinks of as so obviously an advance on the morality and politics of the disintegrating late medieval Christendom that it replaced.

Liberal Morality and Democratic Politics;
Modern Progress?

Liberal morality and democratic politics suffer from the same teleological deficiencies as the Darwinian conception of survival. That is, there is no qualitative or meaningful aim embedded in them that could be aspired toward in order to advance human flourishing. This is an explicit feature of the forms of evaluation and power that are archetypally modern. In philosophical parlance, modern liberalism is designed to advance discrete realms of negative freedom (freedom *from* interference, imposition, regulation) and discrete realms of absolute control (notably, the nation state aspires to a total monopoly of the use of violence). Here there is no *substantial* vision of a *summum bonum*, only a *formal* conception of liberty. So one is free to value and believe whatever one desires to value and believe, and one has, supposedly, value-neutral means of pursuing one's preferences as regulated by legal controls over public order (enforced by the violent power invested in the state). So the "target," the meaningful and valuable *end* toward which one is progressing, the substantive content of a normative vision of human flourishing, is not defined, only the means of "making progress" is defined.

It should be clear enough to observe that modern scientific truth's rejection of metaphysics and theology, and its discourse of objective knowledge grounded in merely empirical evidence and merely mathematical causal dynamics, makes substantive reasoning about valuable and meaningful ends impossible. To the modern mind, only functionally necessary natural needs, and only pleasure- and pain-determined motivations can be considered factual and basic, and higher-order meanings and values are considered constructed glosses on meaningless and valueless natural facts. Higher-order values and meanings can no longer be taken seriously as knowledge claims about truth in higher-order terms (and this makes modernity an advance on medievalism?!). This being the case, the driving ideology of progress within modernity is, in its own terms, a constructed propaganda with no basis in any sort of properly qualitative conception of genuinely meaningful ends worthy of progressing toward.

Even though it is not the case that there could be a meaningful qualitative end defining human flourishing within modernity, nevertheless, the ideology of liberalism posits itself as progress by recourse to the claim that arbitrary and violent coalitions of religious and civic power are irrational and bad, and liberal democracy is rational and good. There is a tacit view of human flourishing here, even if there can be no real grounds for it within a modernity that vigorously excludes the metaphysical and the theological from the factual and the rational. And here, at the level of an ideology, which is widely believed and which informs a range of legal norms, perhaps modernity really does illustrate a genuine advance on medievalism.

But perhaps not. The alliance between recognized civic authorities and the upholding of the status quo via the use of violence has not diminished in the West since the seventeenth century. The establishment of my own nation—Australia—was an exercise in barbaric brutality and rampant violent conquest on a horrifying scale.[4] Modern colonialism was a staggeringly violent abuse of mere superior violent power, and a blatant defiance of liberal and humanitarian Enlightenment values for the conquered and the convicts. Medieval popes have no monopoly on horrifying self-serving enterprises in violent control. Somewhere in the vicinity of 50,000,000 people died in World War Two and tens of millions of ideological murders under Stalin and Mao shows that modern industrial war and the tyrannies of secular modern ideologies act with a brutality and inhumanity that has no parallel in the Middle Ages in terms of the sheer numbers of victims. Greater power in means is not progress just because it is modern social control that is facilitated rather than religio-civic institutional control. And, at the heart of the post-war "free world"—the USA—a culture of enterprising affluence produces an underclass of systemic underprivilege, people who end up in the US's enormous incarceration institutions, a significant proportion of whom are ritually executed on Death Row. This does not excuse medieval brutality and religious violence, but it does point out that such horrifying features of human society have not been superseded just because we are now modern secular rationalists.

---

4. Australian pastoral settlement was astonishingly violent and destructive of the peoples who had lived on the Southern continent for many thousands of years. See Boyce, *1835* for a carefully documented and harrow account of the systemic dispossession, murder, rape, and deadly infection of the Aboriginal peoples of Victoria, such that there was a decline of more than 80 percent in their population between 1835 and 1865.

Is the Loss of the Very Idea of Ontological Knowledge Progress?

Arguments about whether or not modern progress is a coherent idea, and whether it has been practically achieved, can be parried and nuanced on both sides of the ledger ad infinitum. The most fundamental argument against what I have put forward is that we now know that there really is no objective value and meaning in the world. Consequently, we know that an entirely instrumental understanding of knowledge and power and entirely sensually defined conceptions of "good" and "bad" are a genuine advance on philosophically speculative (and untrue) and religiously situated (and untrue) notions of truth, value, meaning, and being. If that were indeed true, then the idea of teleology traced to any sort of non-utilitarian and non-hedonistically measurable criteria would be false and our release from that falsity would be a real enlightenment regarding how things actually are, and hence, genuine progress. According to such a reductively naturalistic account of the virtue of modernity, the loss of ontological thinking is a genuine good, for the ties between ontological fantasies about essence and existence, indemonstrable speculative metaphysics and scientifically unjustifiable and miraculous (that is impossible) theological belief are deep and basic. We have finally come of age—to repeat a slogan of the Enlightenment—and have cast aside the childish dreams of the pre-scientific superstitious imagination of humanity.

An obvious objection to the above is that there can be no conception of progress from medieval times to modern times if reductive naturalism is true, for empirical observation tells us that religious belief concerning the ultimate nature of reality is *just as natural* as metaphysical convictions premised on non-belief in religion. Further, if knowledge is really simply an instrumental construct where all meanings and values are glosses that we generate out of our own cultural imaginations, *ex nihilo*, then the value and meaning of scientific truth can have *no inherent superiority* to religious myth just because it is more instrumentally potent for those in a position to use it. Even if instrumental potency is a function of modern knowledge because that knowledge is a true reflection of the mechanisms of material reality (which it is), it does not necessarily follow (if logic is considered important) that a materialistic and naturalistic account of reality is true, and it *cannot* follow that qualitatively and hermeneutically vacuous scientific truth has *any* real meaning or value (it only has power). So the idea that modernity, with its loss of the very lexicon of meaningful teleology and ontological truth, could be progressive in any *meaningful* sense (for the very idea of progress is tacitly teleological and tacitly ontological) can be safely dismissed.

But let us compare the cultural and political implications of life-worlds in relation to a public arena not defined by ontology and a public arena engaged with ontology. Perhaps we will find some sort of progress here.

Against Public Ontology

The great instrumental advantage of modernity over other life-worlds is its neat functional demarcation between the power structures of a single public and objective, merely factual world of action, natural forces, legal structures, and (ultimately violent) social controls, and the affirmation of pluriform private and subjective belief worlds of personal values, meanings, and teleological aims. This is understood as a life-world where the value of personal liberty, as measured in terms of the lack of a publicly imposed overarching ontological belief and value structure, is strongly upheld. So merely practical public power and discretely personal private freedom define modernity. (Note, these are, naturally enough, very modern conceptions of power and freedom.) This is a life-world generated by the disintegration of the objective from the subjective, the demarcation of facts from meanings, and the separation of power from religious and moral belief/authority. And indeed, measured in terms of amoral technological and public power and subjective personal freedom, this is a much better life-form than life-forms that are relatively integrated across the subject/object divide.

So yes, modernity is better than non-modernity at the things *it* values. And certainly I, as someone born and raised in the modern West, value my personal liberties as much as any other modern person. I also value modern medicine as much as any other person, and appreciate its often stunning curative effectiveness. The personal freedoms and instrumental potencies of modernity are certainly goods integral with this way of life. Even so, it is a rather hubristic false valuation of incommensurate criteria to claim that modernity is better than non-modernity simply because non-modern life-worlds fail to succeed in modern terms.

But let us try to at least partially overcome this incommensurate valuation difficulty by comparing both sets of criteria rather than simply assuming one set. Let us not only judge the technological impotencies and personal liberty infringements of medievalism by the standards of modern power and liberty, but let us also judge the categories of merely instrumental power and private liberty by the standards of a life-world that is more integral of the objective and the subjective.

Is Integration or Demarcation across the Objective/Subjective Divide Better?

With qualified deference to Wittgenstein's incommensurability problem, it must be recognized that there is no hermeneutically impartial way of approaching this question. One will evaluate demarcation as metaphysically and morally deficient from an outlook tending toward integration, and one will evaluate integration as oppressive and impractical from an outlook tending toward demarcation. Even so, this does not necessarily mean that one side of this evaluation cannot be more persuasive than the other side. It certainly doesn't mean that both sides are equally legitimate (though both sides might be equally illegitimate given the three logical alternatives in relation to bivalent truth: X right Y wrong, Y right X wrong, both X and Y wrong or only partially right). Wittgenstein's incommensurability can only justify equal legitimacy (both X and Y are right in relation to their own language games) if different language games of meaning are considered to have no relation to bivalent reality, or no knowable relation to reality, or if reality itself is considered to have no bivalent relationship to any human evaluation. Any of these latter possibilities renders substantively concerned logic and, ultimately, truth-aiming linguistic meaning impossible, so I will not undermine the very idea of meaningful communication by taking radical language game incommensurability seriously. So let us run the comparison between integration and demarcation in both directions under the premise that one of these evaluations may well have a closer relation to truth than the other.

Demarcation is good; integration is bad

Due to a very high valuation on—for want of a better term—the sanctity of the individual, preserving a zone of personal sovereignty in regard to valuations and final commitment loyalties is equated with inward liberty. A corresponding commitment to outward liberty—defining the rules of power in procedural terms, rather than substantive terms—ensures that those with the means of potency (money and/or position) can operate in the world under a stable and relatively fair set of rules toward whatever evaluative ends they desire (provided the means are at least arguably legal). Thus, a neat demarcation between the subjective realm of values, meanings, and personal commitments and the objective realm of facts, instrumental potency, and public actions ensures both liberty and certainty in a manner that makes for happy individuals and powerful public actors.

The pluralism and enterprising dynamism of modernity is astounding. Consumers are presented with an astonishing array of different items, images, and experiences to choose from, according to whatever personal choice valuation they may desire (though their desires are being continually primed and disciplined by advertising). There is a tacit *summum bonum* for the common life here—economic growth—but this, as Friedrich Hayek outlines, is an explicitly non-teleological and merely aggregate pragmatic "end."[5] That is, economic growth has no moral, transcendent, or intellective target, no substantive vision of a common human flourishing. The idea that higher net corporate profits equates to the "good" of greater collective wealth is an explicitly instrumental and materialist measure of "good" that maintains a dogged public silence on all matters of substantive moral quality and spiritual purpose. It is also blind to entrenched corporate privilege and the "two-speed economies" that GDP measurements typically hide.

Compared to medieval conceptions of "just price"—where substantive moral and theological concerns governed markets to some extent— "free market" economics aims to be much more economically efficient. Any society that has publicly framed conceptions of sacredness that are "bigger" than the modern sanctity of the individual's personal valuations is going to be less economically efficient than modernity. This was as true for communist East Germany as it is for the modern Islamic world; and both communism and Islam, as ways of life that see substantive moral and ideological/theological concerns as integral with public concerns, find the global power of modern Western enterprise a corrosive force undermining their capacity to keep their way of being in the world afloat.

Religious, ethical, and "life-style" pluralism are strong features of secular modernity. A clear emphasis on the facts of action, rather than the meaning of actions or the beliefs of actors, governs the public arena in all areas other than sexuality and patriotism. (Though even in sexuality, there is no substantive norm governing sexual behavior other than the sacrosanct principle of freely consenting adults.) So one can believe whatever

5. Hayek, *Road to Serfdom*, 59.

one wants about value and meaning privately, and consenting private relations between individuals are seen as the business of those individuals and no-one else. At the same time, the public discourses of knowledge and power are factual and procedural and, in functional terms, materialist and atheist. That is, moral truth and theological truth are excluded from the public realm as if they do not exist in reality, but only have meaning as freely chosen subjective belief commitments.

So personal freedoms of belief, public economic freedoms, and knowledge and technological power grounded in the objectivity of materially demonstrable facts are seen as the primary goods of Western modernity. These goods are grounded in a strict functional divide between the objective and the subjective. But is this divide a genuine good? And, more fundamentally, is this divide a collectively supported legal fiction that is not even possible in reality?

Integration is good; demarcation is bad

If one has an integral outlook, then changes in our understanding of objective facts will result in changes in an understanding of subjective meanings. This is in fact what happened with the rise of modernity, for we can only notionally demarcate the objective from the subjective because we only ever know the objective "within" our subjective consciousness. In many regards, the life-world isolation of subjective meanings from objective facts is a mechanism that attempts to preserve subjective meanings that are no longer readily integrateable with the notions of mere facticity and non-evaluated use that are basic to the modern scientific perspective. Reductive modern naturalism is a more integral approach to scientific facts and moral and religious meanings than is a secular division between natural reality (which is value- and meaning-free, but materially objective) and the bizarre notion of supernatural "reality," which, because it has no material and objective existence, occupies an optional subjective belief realm where religious "truths" and moral "realities" can still be deemed significant, even though they have no relation to scientific knowledge.

Two things become apparent concerning the functional division between private meaning freedoms and objective facts. Firstly, it does not really work. Secondly, it has the effect of rendering values and meanings unrelated to objective material reality (that is, values and meanings become substantively fictitious, even if they are subjectively significant to those who choose to hold them). This encourages an instrumental pragmatism and an indifference to every substantive belief system of values and meanings. But a third factor also becomes apparent. If all values and meanings are fictitious, then the value and meaning of scientific objectivity is also fictitious, and the scientific conception of objective reality (which we can only know in our subjective consciousness) can no longer be considered a strong truth foundation, it is merely an instrument of power.

So I cannot see that this modern separation of facts from meanings, the separation of quantity from quality, the separation of heaven from earth, the displacement of a system of meaningful purposes in human life and nature by a merely mathematically predictable understanding of physical necessities, is progress. It doesn't actually work—for subjectivity and objectivity are integral in our experience of reality—and this *loss* of integrative understanding tends toward amoral instrumental pragmatism. This type of power has no genuine regard for truth or essential meaning, but has a heightened interested in morally un-inhibited power and the mass propagation of useful fictions.

This leads us to the central pathology of modernity; *morally and theologically uninhibited instrumental power without meaning or value.* (This is a pathology of power rather than a pathology of modernity as such, but there has never been so much power available to be pathological with, and so little religious or philosophical restraint within a cultural life-world as there is in modernity.) That this is pathological is clearly visible in the relation of high finance to politics within late modernity.

The only objective measure of value the life-world of instrumental modernity can now collectively agree on is financial. Yet financial value is a very peculiar species of "value." Firstly, for an empirical age, it is curious that money has no physical existence. It is a type of "value"—"exchange value"—that is purely numerical. In a sense, high finance shows us the manner in which the abstract mathematical side of modernity is able to shake off the empirical material side of modernity altogether. Secondly, as a merely quantitative and instrumental type of "value," financial power is explicitly non-teleological, amoral, and—in itself—meaningless. As such, financial power is entirely unresponsive to the imperatives, meanings, and rationality of civically concerned political power. This was seen very dramatically in the 2015 dealings between the first term of Syriza government in Greece and the "troika" of financial institutions (the European Central Bank, the European Commission, and the International Monetary Fund).

At the 27 June 2015 Eurogroup meeting it was unavoidably clear that the democratic processes, political decisions, and economic realities of the Greek polity had no leverage at all in its "negotiations" with the troika. As it turns out, the matter is very simple; when financial institutions deal with insolvent polities, whoever has the money determines the rules, the conditions, and the outcome. Human and economic realities and political processes are irrelevant to financial power. The Eurogroup only *appears* to be a political and economic policy interface between the financial institutions and the member states of the Eurozone so that the states could determine their future together. In fact, the Eurogroup has no constitution and no binding governance regulations, and yet it has more power to shape the economic fortunes of EU member states than most of those states have within their own polities. The reality is that nationally elected finance ministers within the Eurogroup are all dictated to by the unelected power-brokers of the troika, such that the Eurogroup *could not* deviated from imposing impossible austerity and unachievable repayment conditions on Greece in 2015. Even though the economic evidence was indisputable that the trajectory pursued by the troika since 2009 had done nothing but deepen Greece's economic dysfunction and had made it impossible for the Greek government to ever repay the loans, the economic realities and political determinations of a state within the Eurozone were here obviously entirely irrelevant to the "necessities" of democratically unaccountable high finance. Fiscal power proved impervious to economic reality, entirely unresponsive to humanitarian need, and utterly ignored the political will of the Greek people in electing Syriza to re-negotiate the terms of its dealings with the troika.[6] On 5 June 2015 the referendum in Greece delivered a resounding "No" to the troika's austerity demands and the resultant economic implosion of the Greek state, but this had no impact on financial power, which had already shut the Greek banking system down.

Even in the premier democratic state of the "free world"—the USA—power is centered in high finance and wealthy corporate lobbyists. The multiple millions of dollars necessary to run as a presidential candidate locates all candidates in a relation of dependence on the interests of wealthy donors. (Donald Trump, as super-rich in his own right, could claim independence from the interests of Big Money; but this is an astonishing irony.)

6. See Syriza's finance minister, Yanis Varoufakis, respond to the breakdown of Eurogroup negotiations between Greece and the troika here: http://yanisvaroufakis.eu/2015/06/28/as-it-happened-yanis-varoufakis-intervention-during-the-27th-june-2015-eurogroup-meeting/.

This intimate relationship between lucrative lobbyists and politicians in Washington tucks the political system in neatly with corporate power. The idea that the common citizens of American rule themselves, and for themselves, is nothing but an idea. They are ruled *by* an international moneyed elite, and *for* that international moneyed elite, as are we all. The natural degradation of civic consciousness to the advancement of the self-interests of the powerful, under a "realism" of instrumental power within modernity, is here played out in stark terms. Democracy is a mere ideology now. Our states serve elite transnational financial power now, and that power has no intrinsic interest in civic issues, but is only concerned to expand its own meaningless financial power, with as little moral, legal, environmental, and national limitations as possible.[7]

Conclusion

I cannot see that the loss of integrative thinking between what are now considered subjective meanings and values on the one hand, and public and objective facts and instrumental power on the other hand, is progress. A key aspect of this modern transition away from a more integral life-world understanding of the relation between facts and meanings is the loss of the very idea of being. Ontology makes no sense to us any more, for ontology grounds our understanding of reality in an inherently meaningful notion of existence, situated between meaningful and transcendent essence "above" existence, and transient and contingent imminence "below" existence. In contrast, modernity is premised on a univocally material "reality" where the separation of objective facts from subjective meanings and the tacit assertion of an anti-ontology of meaningless constructivism, gives a free hand to "amoral" instrumental power.

The forgetfulness of being is an inherently bad development in the history of Western culture for it frees staggering instrumental power from moral, meaningful, and theological restraint. This development equips the power elites of the modern world with a hubristic indifference to the true realities of existence and actively legitimates oppressive and destructive power as somehow simply necessary and "realistic."

---

7. See George, *Shadow Sovereigns*; Klein, *The Shock Doctrine*; Ferguson, *Inside Job*; Shaxson, *Treasure Islands*.

5

RE-UNDERSTANDING KNOWING
AND BELIEVING

The modern world arises out of a new approach to knowing and believing, an approach that isolates knowledge to the realm of mathematics and repeatable empirical evidence and that cordons theological and
moral belief convictions off from the objective reality of its knowledge
discourse. The ancient discourse of ontology is lost in this development.
Today we are at an interesting juncture because while the fictitious nature
of modern truth discourses are now well understood—thanks to counter-
Enlightenment, hermeneutic philosophy and various postmodern critiques
of the metanarrative of modern scientific truth—the power of the modern
life-world has never been more pervasive. In effect, what has happened is
that whilst an Enlightenment view of modernity is now recognized to be
impossibly philosophically naïve, so powerful is the mythos of modern
scientific truth that we cannot really believe that knowing and believing
can be integrated with a meaningful understanding of reality (ontology
proper). We have turned functionally skeptical and nihilistic regarding any
meaningful knowledge of reality because the modern approach to seeking
to generate such an outlook has failed.

The time has come to seriously consider returning to an integral
understanding of meaningful truth, to recover ontology. Yet this can only
be realistically contemplated if we are prepared to re-think the nature of

knowing and believing that is native to the modern life-world. In this chapter we will seek to re-think knowledge and belief in such a manner that it could be integral with a meaningful ontology of reality.

Meaningful Knowledge

There is no escaping the pre-existence of meaning to any enterprise in knowing. Yet so deeply ingrained is the modern (and impossible) attempt to ground meaning in knowing, that no genuine appreciation of the foundational reality of meaning seems to penetrate the modern conception of truth. In this section I will seek to show firstly; that meaning is the foundation of knowing; secondly, that there is no credible reason to assume that because meaning cannot be derived from modern knowing that meaning is not real and cannot be true; thirdly, that only by taking the reality of meaning seriously could knowing (and believing) be valid; and fourthly, that once we can seriously think of knowing as grounded in meaning, this will radically revise our conception of what knowing truth actually is.

Meaning is Foundational to Knowing

All the hard leg work demonstrating that meaning is always prior to knowing has been done by linguistic philosophers in the trajectory of Hamann, post-critical thinkers working in Michael Polanyi's trajectory, hermeneutic philosophers working in Gadamer's trajectory, and contemporary "Continental" scholars of classical epistemology working in Lloyd Gerson's trajectory. I will very briefly rehearse these arguments now.

The priority of meaning over knowing is not a *temporal* or *material* priority, nor is it some non-sensory rationalism or intuitive revelation that is discrete from sensory knowledge. Rather, along Kantian lines, firstly it is the recognition that for knowledge to be meaningful in the mind of the knower, structures of meaning must be hard-wired into the way we perceive the spatio-temporal sensory field. But secondly, and more radically than Kant, Hamann points out that our meaningful thoughts about the perceived world are always embedded in language, which pre-exists the particular thinker and can never be adequately understood in terms of "pure" Kantian apriori epistemic structures. The larger social and historical context of language is always prior to every mature interpretation of sensory data. Knowledge is embedded in cultural and historically evolving meanings and, Hamann argues, in the divine mystery of meaning itself. No meaningful communication of thought is possible without language. That is, while syntax can be analyzed in a positivist manner, there is no simply empirically or mechanistically reductive explanation for semantics. Semantics is the living sacrament of the primal reality of meaning itself, which the structures and mechanisms of language carry. If one does not take semantics as prior to syntax in understanding what language itself is, then everything reduces to merely mechanistic syntax and the very idea of meaningfully studying the nature, the meaning, and the essence of language becomes incoherent. Such an observation does not negate the indispensable role of syntax in language, but it places the grammatical means of communication as a lower-order function of semantics itself. A good structural and material appreciation of the expressive dependence of higher semantic meanings on lower syntaxical functions is not here disputed, but such an appreciation in no manner negates—for Hamann—the *ontological* dependence of the lower on the higher. Thus, Hamann refuses the incoherent reduction of semantics to syntax. Thirdly, the relationships, communities, political structures, economic practices, religious assumptions, and moral norms of the context of spoken meaning are always prior to any meaningful interpretation of what is said in the context of genuine communication. Knowledge is always constructed in relational contexts within communities that use specific languages with their inbuilt meanings. These contexts are prior to the entry of any particular knower/speaker. Fourthly, classical epistemology holds—very credibly—that meaning must be prior to knowing, not only for any knowing to be meaningful, but for there to be any knowers, and even anything at all to know. Here again—and contrary to reductively materialist modern assumptions—mind is higher, and hence ontologically prior, to matter. Let us dwell on this fourth point briefly.

Mind is prior to matter: the wisdom of ancient epistemology

Simply put, the ancients maintained that unless you assume that the reality of meaning is fundamental to the cosmos, all thought, reasoning, and language is ultimately meaningless. The idea that it makes any reasoned sense to adhere to the pure poetic constructivism of hermeneutic nihilism is the most fundamental error of thinking it is possible to perform. The ancients did not make this error because they took thinking and meaningful communication seriously, and they took the reality of purposive and rational order—"mind"—in the cosmos seriously. Here meaning or mind is the grounds out of which all beings that exist within an obviously ordered cosmos arise. The premise of the ancients was that ordered material reality can only arise from mind and that non-ordered non-meaningful reality did not actually (and could not) exist. The objectivity of *Logos* (meaning, reason, communicable intelligence) in the cosmos could obviously not exist if there were only mere mindless material things. Because of this premise, the ancients took qualitative distinctions seriously such that higher order functions—thought, the mind—could not be explained in terms of lower order functions that were of a different qualitative nature, such, to use a modern example, as the snapping of synapses. Thinking like an ancient within a modern context, it is entirely reasonable to hold that the higher order functions of the mind are physically dependent on the material operations of the brain, but it makes no logical or empirical sense to maintain that material dependence entails qualitative equivalence or that mere quantitative complexity produces qualitative distinctions. Modernists tend to try to obliterate qualitative distinctions and try to explain the higher in the terms of the lower because we hold to a progressive "Darwinian" reductivism where the higher is always derived from and explained by the lower, and where the lower is always the primal reality.[1] But how reasonable are our "Darwinian" assumptions?[2]

If you look at any natural phenomena you will observe mind boggling structural and relational complexity that can only exist and function within the context of ordered reality because of the actual existence of order, purpose, and meaning in reality. Take, at random, the seed pod of the tree *Tipuana tipu*. This South American tree has seed pods that are delicately weighted wings that rotate like a helicopter blade, and can fly considerable distances, when a gust of wind lifts them from the tree. To deduce

1. Modernists typically try to derive meaning as a function of sensory perception as if mere sensation produces intellection. Aquinas' famous rendition of Aristotelian epistemology explains that there is "nothing is in the intellect that was not previously in sense" (*Quaestiones Disputatae de Veritate*, Question 2, Article III, 19), yet this is no refutation of the ontological priority of intelligibility over perception. Aquinas found perception the indispensable *medium* of intellection for us, but the priority of the intellective in the order of reality is taken as given by both Aristotle and Aquinas. For Aquinas, it is the gifting of essence to all beings by God that makes perceived reality intelligible and this makes perception and knowledge both possible in the first place, and—most basically—a means of communion with God.

2. Here I am interested in "Darwinian" ideas as cosmologically orienting philosophical assumptions embedded in modern reductive epistemic commitments.

that non-thinking mere chance mutations plus the inherently meaningless survivalist dynamics of natural selection plus vast eons of time produces this phenomena is *necessary* for us moderns because modern practical reasoning is embedded in a theoretical commitment to non-meaningful matter being the primal reality out of which all natural phenomena arise. So, to us, the non-thinking tree produces an artefact of astonishing beauty and subtle aerodynamic proficiency entirely by survivalistically convenient genetic accident and entirely without the guidance or intention of mind. (I wonder what the science of evolutionary biological development would look like if we took mind in the cosmos seriously.) But the irony of this is that if such astonishingly sophisticated artificing as done by the Tipuana tipu tree just happens without mind, then it is inductively obvious that *human thought and our own minds too* (and their inductive theories about the primacy of matter) *are accidental products of non-thinking, non-meaningful reality*. If this is the case, then deduction itself is a chance product of meaningless matter that has no necessary meaning, and reason itself is not in reality, but only "exists" within that most allusive of all epiphenomena of matter, the internal consciousness of our brains. Reasoning from within an epistemic framework embedded in a tacit and instrumental cosmology of primal matter, our knowledge, for all we subjectively "know," can have no real meaning that transcends the structures and interpretations that our minds meaninglessly impose on our experience.

If meaning and thought are only functions of our internal consciousness and are not evident in the cosmos as a whole, and do not signify that reality itself is a function of rational and meaningful mind, *then our commitment to Darwinian reductivism is itself meaningless and without any necessary basis in reality*. Thus, we can see that the ancients were correct to maintain that no serious thought can succeed without taking the existence of mind as a primal reality in the cosmos seriously.

Just Because Meaning Cannot Be Derived from Modern Knowing Does Not Mean That Meaning Is Not Real and Cannot Be True

Around two thousand years ago, Middle Platonism was the dominant philosophical trajectory of the ancient Greco-Roman world. This is a type of philosophy that can be readily integrated with religion, or that can provide its own theology, aesthetic practices, and spiritual disciplines in place of institutionally organized religion. The Cappadocian church fathers and

Augustine demonstrate the manner in which the Christian religion integrated significant features of Middle Platonism and Neoplatonism into Christian theology and practice. Plotinus demonstrates the manner in which Neoplatonism can be an explicit alternative to Christian Platonism, as a more philosophically "pure" theology. The plethora of gnostic cults that arose in late classical times also illustrate the manner in which esoteric and semi-philosophical knowledge combined with cultic secrets were readily integrated with the quest for personal salvation. By the late classical era, the rise of imperially backed Christian religion tied broadly Platonist theological philosophy in with Christian doctrine, the Christian cultus, and the Roman imperium. When the late Roman civilization collapsed in the sixth century AD, much of what was left of high culture and the late classical religio-imperial alliance lay dormant in the West in the Vatican. Yet a passionate interest in the lives of the saints, the vitality of monastic orders, and the stunning advances of Celtic missionaries were astonishingly effective in the very dark age of barbarian invasion and inter-city-state anarchy characteristic of much of Europe between the sixth and the tenth centuries. When Europe recovered in the twelfth century, the old Christian imperium (but with the "emperor" at second fiddle to the pope) was somewhat revived, and the integration of philosophy and what we would now call science with theology and Christian doctrine was taken for granted. But the emerging merchant class, the wealth and military power of the aristocracy, and scholarship within the new universities also arose with the revival of Western Europe, such that money, power, and knowledge were not simply integral with the church, but were also vying for their own spheres of control. The manner in which William of Ockham champions the separation of ecclesial power from "secular" matters (though for entirely theological reasons) in the fourteenth century shows that the attempt to delineate religion from other spheres of knowledge and power is deeply embedded in the medieval world, even though that world was astonishingly integral as regards religion and all other spheres of life when compared to modern secularism.

The point I am making with this brief historical sketch is that the idea that philosophy and knowledge was independent of theology, religion, and power was not functionally viable within the life-world of Western Europe from late classical times right up until the seventeenth century, even though the pathways toward disintegration are laid down centuries before the seventeenth century. Modernity's great experiment has been to create—really for the first time—the notion of secular philosophy and secular knowledge, which at least aims to be entirely independent of ecclesial authority and political interest. Faith and reason have been separated out such that knowledge and reason have been tied together as concerned with merely objective facticity, logical coherence, and "merely" instrumental (as opposed to political) power on the one hand, and religion, values, and the interpretation of meanings has been tied together and cordoned off from the world of objective knowledge and political power, and given over to the realm of subjective personal freedom. The grand narrative of modernity is that this development is progress. Which is to say that there is a tacit normative commitment to the separation of knowledge from meaning and theology such that any attempt to integrate these spheres is simply assumed to be regressive and an impossible attempt to return to some now long-displaced and inherently oppressive mode of thinking and being in the world. What this means is that if meaning and reason themselves dissolve under the impact of the demarcations of modernity (as has happened), our tacit normative life-world commitment to the "progressive" nature of modernity makes it very hard to think that there now *could* be any meaningful knowledge of reality; knowledge is now *only* manipulative power. But, this reflexive inclination is just that; there is no necessary reason why the failure of modernity to produce justified true belief that is merely factual and merely logical means that a meaningful knowledge of reality which is premised on the integration of knowing, being, and faith is not possible. Let me rephrase that sentence in a few steps.

1. The attempt to establish indubitable epistemological foundations for objective scientific knowledge was never actually possible, socioculturally or hermeneutically, and has now clearly failed philosophically.

2. A consequence of the failure mentioned in 1 above is that the assumption that "only experimentally demonstrable ratio-empirical knowledge warrants the designation as true knowledge" cannot be philosophically supported.

3. The notion that "if an objectivist, secular, non-metaphysically premised, and hermeneutically impartial knowledge cannot be had, then truth cannot be had" can only be supported by the dogged commitment to the philosophically failed premises of modern epistemological foundationalism. Such commitment undermines the alleged objectivity and demonstrability of the distinctly modern approach to knowledge.

4. The attempt to reframe modern philosophy as skeptical, pragmatic, as merely grammatical as regards mathematics/logic/semantics, and as merely instrumental as regards positive science, does not provide any strong grounds of rejecting the integrative understanding of knowledge, ontology, and faith that modernity displaced. That is, modern skepticism is based on the *belief commitment* that maintains that it is impossible to know truth *because* it is impossible for us to demonstrate the foundational warrants of our knowledge (i.e., this stance is negatively committed to modern epistemological foundationalism). Yet, if reason is prior to our knowledge, and if revelation from the divine grounds of reason reaches down into and undergirds our epistemic field, but is not itself "native" to that field, then there is no necessary reason why our failure to demonstrate the foundations of our own knowledge implies the impossibility of a real, though analogical, participation of our minds in truth.

5. The modern commitment to rule the possibility of revelation out of knowledge cannot be supported by its own instrumental skepticism. Indeed, no skepticism can support its own skeptical commitments. No attempt at a thoroughly negative belief commitment can escape fundamental internal incoherence; the only belief commitment that does not implode is a positive one. That is, *faith* rather than doubt is the only coherent grounds of *any* belief commitment where fundamental warrants cannot be demonstrated, as is always, finally, the case.

Given the above, it is clear that the "postmodern" stance powerfully advocated by Foucault that because all forms of knowing, believing, interpreting, and acting are intimately political and interested, then only political interests are finally "real" to us, is actually a strangely unjustified commitment to the modern project. Foucault himself, in rejecting the label postmodern, seems sensibly aware of his continuity with modernity. For the continuation of modern thinking once its foundations are known to be indemonstrable—along Foucault's lines—only implies atheism, constructivism, and the reduction of knowledge and belief to power if there is a decisive existential commitment to epistemological nihilism premised on the failure of modern epistemological foundationalism. What this stance does not consider, however, is that grounding knowledge in ontology and revelation—as per the Neoplatonist classical mainstream and patristic and

Augustinian Christendom—is shown to be inherently *more* credible than epistemological nihilism in the light of the philosophical failure of modernity. That is, epistemological nihilism cannot be meaningfully committed to *any* knowledge as true, and *this undermines the truth of epistemological nihilism itself*, whereas an understanding of meaningful knowledge premised on a revealed partial grasp of ontologically meaningful reality implies no internal contradiction.

Foucault's stance shows the sort of existential commitment to the truth of final absurdity that is quite natural for a stance *continuous* with the failure of modern epistemological foundationalism. But such a stance also implies the meaninglessness of Foucauldian critique, or that such critique is itself merely an exercise in power, and not an exercise in truth (and that, impossibly, it is true that there is no truth and that all knowledge is only a function of power). In the final analysis, an existential commitment to epistemological nihilism, simply out of continuity with the secular objectivist and scientistically rationalist habits of the modern life-form, is *entirely unjustifiable philosophically*, and any alternative belief outlook of real meaning cannot be *known* to be false by an epistemological nihilist.

Only By Taking the Existence of Meaning Seriously Could Knowing (and Believing) Be Valid

Above I have sought to point out that the determination to continue the modern trajectory after it is clear that modern epistemological foundationalism could not succeed is a voluntarist act of existential absurdism, which inherently denies the very enterprise of rational truth-seeking and *can* have no meaningful argument against any form of rational and qualitative realism. The inverse of this stance is also true. If there is meaningful truth that can be, in some measure, known by us, then not only must modern epistemological foundationalism be found impossible, but the pathway of epistemological nihilism implied by continuation in the modern trajectory must also be abandoned. Yet, whether knowing and meaning is actually valid, actually has some genuine relation to meaningful truth, is not implied just by reversing the late modern existential commitment to epistemological nihilism. Here I am not arguing that truth-related epistemology is necessarily implied by the philosophical failure of modern epistemological foundationalism, rather I am arguing that only by rejecting epistemological nihilism *could* a meaningful knowledge of truth be possible.

The significance of this is that reasoning toward truth is always a *good-faith* enterprise premised on the freely chosen rejection of radical epistemological nihilism. Knowledge of the true is not even potentially viable without this good faith. Hence, epistemology, ontology, and faith must be considered integral, and the very idea of modern truth is problematic in these terms from the outset. So while we might indeed have no final means of knowing whether our knowledge is finally true, that is an entirely different position than claiming that because we cannot produce the warrants of sensory and rational truth within the field of sensory and rational demonstration then there is no truth to be known (as far as our knowledge is concerned) such that all knowledge is *really* always a constructivist manipulative tool in its essence. But note here, this presumed ontology of knowledge—that knowledge is *really* instrumental power—is unjustifiable within the dysfunctional warrants of failed modern epistemological foundationalism. So not only could knowledge only be true if we have good faith in meaningful knowledge itself (while refusing to accept that knowledge is capable of providing its own warrants), but there is something profoundly disingenuous about the tacit ontology of an explicitly non-ontological commitment to epistemological nihilism.

Rethinking Knowing, Ontology, Believing, and Truth as Integral with Each Other

The biggest difficulty that faces us if we do not want to be continuous with the failed enterprise of modern epistemological foundationalism, is that the modern life-world simply assumes that the only concept of "truth" that is valid is a merely objectivist, merely instrumental, merely rational conception of truth. That is, modern truth is tied to a specific notion of "the facts," is considered valid if "it works," and valid reasoning is understood as a function of merely procedural logic, which is seen as discrete from substantive (understood as entirely poetic) meanings and values. As outlined above, there is, and can be, no modern epistemological foundationalist demonstration of the validity of this stance. Indeed, this stance implies its own destruction because its implied ontology of pure nature (modern materialism) does not see mind and good as primary and qualitative realities that are an objective feature of the cosmos, hence reason is simply a function of meaningless matter of no intrinsic good, such that only instrumental power serving non-rational (instinctive) "purposes" is held to really exist. If that is "true" then there is no good and genuinely intellective reason for *anything*, let alone the giving of credence to a good reasoned argument semantically expressed by any human mind. So how then might we re-consider knowledge itself in terms that are not tied to these meaningless and valueless conceptions of "the facts," of "it works," and of a correct mechanical "procedure" of sentence constructions?

Let it be absolutely clear that I intend no dispensing with facts, use, and procedural rigor, rather what we are after is a way to make facts, use, and logic *visible* again, as meaningful and richly true. What I am seeking to do here is revive the classical *priority of ontology* over science, logic, and power, so that science, logic, and power might be substantively meaningful in terms that are genuinely hermeneutically rich and hence existentially recognizable as *meaningful* realities within the world as our *actual* existence experiences it. Within modernity we abstract and extract the kernel of "mere facts" from the husk of cultural embedded meanings, we abstract and extract the kernel of "mere use" from husk of qualitative purpose, and we abstract and extract the kernel of "mere grammatical syntax" from the husk of substantive semantic reasons. Hence, the vision of reality and knowledge we get after this abstraction and extraction is foreign to the world as we actually experience it. Within postmodernity we reduce not only meaning, quality, and semantics to meaningless, mindless tools of power, but science, logic, language, and power also to the reductive and "refined" terms of the modern abstraction. But substantive meanings, quality that is non-reducible to quantity and mere expediency, and "objective" reason (mind in the cosmos) are unavoidably entangled in every aspect of our conscious existence. Both modernity and postmodernity are strangely blind to that which is *existentially obvious*, and that which is impossible to delineate out from facts, use, and syntax. How can we return to the reality of a meaningful cosmos when we have abstracted meaning out of the cosmos and are now addicted in the very structures of the life-world of modern technological society to the "merely" instrumental power that modernity has put into our hands? We have become addicted to an abstracted and refined conception of reality that is at fundamental odds with the existential realities of meaning and value embedded in the lives we actually live.

To make it clear, if we think of facts as having real meanings (even though we may only be able to partially know what those meanings are), if we think of use as always situated within a context of qualitative reality (even though the only qualitative meanings we can articulate and build communities with are in many regards generated by our communities), if we think of meaning itself as a feature of reality (even though any logos we can articulate is always smaller than the Logos of reality itself) then we will understand true knowledge in a very different way to how modernity understands it, and we will not be obliged to follow the semantic implosions inherent in modernity down the postmodern track of epistemological nihilism. And yet, what such a conception of true knowledge might look like is currently very hard for us to think of. It is hard because, against all philosophical evidence to the contrary, we still believe that pragmatic use and mere syntactical logic equates to a proof of objective truth. The idea that truth is only ever accessed, and only ever existentially encountered, within the arms of belief, within the mystery of being, still strikes us as impossible. But not only is it possible, it is unavoidable. Let us try to think of what it means to believe truth, to know within the arms of belief, and to situate facts within the meanings in which they are known to us as our actual existence gives the meaning of facts to us.

The Truth of Being, and Believing the Truth

Now that we are concluding this essay, let us seek to think of ontology as primary, of epistemology as grounded in ontology, and of "good faith" and "right belief" in a meaningful ontology as the premise of any movement toward true knowledge.

Visioning Ontology as Primary

To recover astonishment with being as the grounds of thinking about the meaning of reality is to bring us back to our actual lived experience of reality and to escape the delusional pull of modern abstract instrumental and meaningless power. This is a recovery of wonder itself. For is it not wonderful to be? And is it not wonderful that the cosmos *is* and that we are all in relations of mutual dependence with a vast array of other beings all situated within a universe that is united by a common Logos? This is the immediate reality of conscious and communicable human experience, and all lived human realities are actually situated within this immediate consciousness of ontological wonder. When Jesus of Nazareth said "unless you change and become like children you will never enter the kingdom of heaven" (Matt 18:3) and "no one can see the kingdom of God without being born from above" (John 3:3) surely he is counselling a return, in adulthood, and via reception to divine gift, to primal wonder seen most naturally in a very young child. The safe and loved child is free within the relationships of care into which she is born, and the world is alive with meaning and wonder to her. Something goes wrong in the community or the child if the child does not grow up in a meaning-secure context that enables that person to contribute to the good of the society to which she belongs. Some of the things that go wrong is formation in a culture of competitive struggle for dominance and the experience of power relations defined by violence and exploitation. These things arise because communities and individuals forget the primal wonder of being and respond to the cosmos as "other" and against them, and so are driven by fear and greed, rather than love and generosity.

One of the great means of inoculating ourselves against *metanoia* (conversion: a life-orientating change of mind) that would lead us back to wonder and the meaning and value of actual reality, is the preference for possibility, simulation, escapist fantasy, and the solipsistic illusions of private power embedded in virtuality, over actuality. Awareness of the real naturally leads the open heart to wonder; look at any young child. But we are technologically insulated from being physically present to the reality in which we actually live by a thousand dazzling enchantments now.

The other day I travelled 1800 km to hear a very fine speaker address a small gathering of highly committed and intelligent people drawn from all over my country. On the two hour flight there, I did not look out the window or talk to the iPad-operating person sitting next to me, but buried myself in my computer. This was normal; iPads, computers, and various other "flight mode" derives were in almost every seat. Very few books, very few extended conversations. Then, in the bus from the airport to the city, several strategically placed TVs were going for the entire trip, advertising tourist destinations. Again, I hardly talked to anyone and hardly looked out the window to see where I actually was, and nearly everyone was on their device anyway. In the actual event that I attended, the speaker was world class, and yet about one quarter of the small group of paying, committed, travelled listeners had their phones on and were continuously looking at their devices and note taking or recording—or texting, or social media posting—during the event. To be present and fully attentive to where we are and with whom we are, and at the time we are, is becoming increasingly outside of our very mode of being in the world. Technology is not in any way innocent in this.

Try to do one day without a mobile phone, without getting onto the internet or social media, and just be present and attentive to the people and the places where you actually are. I am not sure that we are even capable of such a child-like sense of being present to the world in which we actually live anymore.

The more magical, powerful, entertaining, and overcoming of the natural boundaries of space and time our technologies become, the more discipline we need in using them if we are to stay grounded in the actual reality in which we live. The easier it is for social media to replace the stubborn realities of actual relationships with neatly presented "information" for and "marketed presentations" of the self, the more caution we need if we are to avoid reducing relationships to instrumental self-promotion opportunities. The more information we can access, the more tempted we will be to assume that information equates to knowledge such that meaning and wisdom become obsolete, and that a large quantity of information somehow equates to a higher quality of information. And, of course, there is a sinister side to the relationships between money, power, and the technologies of information and virtuality. A technologically atomized polity can be weaned off traditional community structures embedded in a moral and spiritual vision of reality, such that the "morality," "spirituality," and the politics of consumerism can be liberated from constraint. The realities of actual relationships can be airbrushed over and we can have a "personal" morality and spirituality that has the very minimum of concrete, continuous, and disciplined commitments to other people. The self becomes the center and the seven deadly sins of Christendom become, all so easily, the seven cardinal virtues of consumerism.

The point I want to draw out here is that because ontology—the wonder and reality of being, and of being who, were, and when we are in relation with other real beings, with being itself, and with the grounds of being—is occluded by modern knowing and doing, the path that consumer virtuality is leading us on looks exciting to us. Indeed, the re-configuring of social reality away from religious, moral, political, economic, and actual reality and toward the financialization of power (the ultimate virtualization of power), the escapist entertainment of the masses, and the unfettered freedoms of our transnational corporate elites at the cost of the degrading exploitation of the poor and the biosphere itself, all this seems like exciting progress to those who will "gain" from this reconfiguration, and who thus continuously propagandize the rest of us to be willing partners in this brave new world. We are conditioned to assume that things are getting better for us because our phones are fancier, even if most of us now live with relentlessly insecure incomes, crippling housing prices, and no impact on the high global power dynamics, which are eroding our actual communities, that our politicians now simply serve.

If we were to be more present to the human and physical environment in which we actually live, if we were to seek to have some genuine say—within humanly scaled local communities—over the conditions in which we actually live, things could be different to what they *actually* are. If we were more aware of the wonder of being, of actual being, this would work against atomization, this would work against the erosion of humanly scaled living institutions; extended family, local church, local school, local community. But the loss of an awareness of being means that actuality is less important to us such that it is strangely "progressive" to be liberated from all the old ways of being concretely grounded in actual meaning, in actual relationships, in actual creation where we live.

To vision ontology as primary is to return to the concrete, the actual, and the existential reality in which we dwell. To vision ontology as primary is to be touched by the reality of real relationships with real people and the real location in which we live, and to become aware of the qualitative and the transcendent as features of the concrete and the actual. The opposite is the case where we abandon being. Fascinated with mere quantity and mathematical abstraction—the "factual" lens of modern science—we filter out value and transcendence from the actual, and we subordinate the actual to the possible as we calculatize reality in order to bend it to the instrumentalism of mere manipulative power.

Visioning Epistemology as Grounded in Ontology

The conception of knowledge as merely quantitative and mathematical is at the center of modernity's distinctly abstract, amoral, and instrumental approach to power. This knowledge is morally meaningless, for when only sensory impressions define valid knowledge then, as Hume saw, "is" does not imply "ought." This knowledge is teleologically primitive, for when "survival" is considered to be the sole objective purpose of living beings, purpose becomes meaningless, for survival in itself has no meaning. Indeed, this sort of knowledge treats all interpretations that are not quantitative and mathematical as subjective constructs, rather than as real. So the transcendent and the qualitative are removed from the realm of knowledge.

Where astonishment with being is the grounds of knowing, things look very different. Knowing grounded in the wonder that there is anything at all grounds knowledge in a value outlook of abundance and delight. Openness to wonder orientates the knower as being within a reality that the knower did not create, that the knower is gifted to be within, and where the knower is part of a meaningful cosmos. Wonder itself is a function of meaning. But wonder is not masterable such that the dialectic between the known and the unknown, between immediacy and mystery, between the increase in knowledge and the increase in wonder is not overcome. And here true knowledge is inseparable from love, such that mere mastery can never be the final purpose of knowledge.

There is an epistemological difference between the knowledge outlook of love and the knowledge outlook of fear. The complexity, unpredictability, and danger of reality may cause fear, or at least appropriate respect, and knowledge is a significant tool in gaining some degree of mastery over one's own immediate environment. Where success at mastery via knowledge becomes defined by the desire for safety and potency, then we develop an outlook of epistemic fear and domination. A forgetfulness of the wonder of ontic donation, and hence of the sense of there being an ontic donor, is the motive toward hubris. This hubris is a false infatuation with epistemic and instrumental mastery aimed at securing unassailable safety and unlimited potency. The driver of this hubris is fear that forgets wonder, power that forgets meaning beyond itself, and the desire for safety that forgets inherent inter-dependence within the material cosmos.

The grounding of knowing in being is the key to recovering an epistemology of love. Here fear is mitigated with trust, epistemic and instrumental mastery is situated in ongoing dialogue with the un-masterable (the sacred), and the experience of dependency and the contingent nature of the conditions that further our interests is not seen as a challenge to be overcome, but as a feature of a cosmos characterized by harmonies of difference, mutualities of the interests of beings, and an undergirding divine mind of goodness and love out of which all beings arise and in which the intelligibility of being itself has its ground.

The reductive gaze of modern knowledge sees only quantity and mathematical and mechanistic relations. This very conveniently frees instrumental power from moral or sacral restraint. Overcoming vulnerability is the great promise of modern technology. Control and power is the promise of the scientific revolution. And yet meaning, mind, the wonder of being, essential purpose, and transcendent significance become invisible to this epistemic gaze. Here power and control readily become the tools of unprecedented technologically enabled oppression and destruction. Fear breeds destruction and oppression and power makes this fear catastrophic.

It is an interesting feature of cosmologies that where there is an empire there is typically a cosmology of primal struggle and redemptive violence embedded in the religion of a ruling class, a class that sees itself as divine. The Marduk cultus of ancient Babylon is a good example of this. When the origin of the cosmos is understood in terms of war and the struggle for conquest, then the powerful see themselves as divine simply because they have dominant power. Plato, notably, upholds the piety of the many local cults of ancient Greece, but without believing that divinity has the same immoral, dominating characteristics as human tyrants, as depicted by the many religious poets of ancient Greece. Likewise, the cosmogenic myth[3] in the Hebrew Scriptures is one of primal harmony, which becomes damaged, but remains, in essence, good, such that royal power in Israel always has to put up with the critique of the prophets when kings abrogate total control to themselves and act in their own interests at the expense of the poor, the alien, and the needy, or set up idols to their own dominance, knowledge, and potency and worship them. Interestingly, the relationship between a Darwinian outlook of domination and survival is tied in with the nineteenth-century British capitalist revolution, which itself arises out of a distinctive theological fixation with total power. The influential ideas of Thomas Hobbes[4] and Adam Smith[5] arise out of a voluntarist conception of God as absolutely powerful and totally unhindered. Francis Bacon is explicit in naming our likeness to God as a likeness in terms of total power over the field of nature given to us by divine mandate. The idea that we are

3. I do not use "myth" here to mean an interpretive meaning narrative which is "factually fictitious." Nor do I use "myth" here to mean a statement of history that is "factually true." The notion of neatly separating out objective historical facts from interpretive, linguistic, and cultural meanings is a feature of distinctly modern mathematico-experimental knowledge, which I am here calling into question. Interpretive meanings and factual truths always exist within each other, even when we say that some meaning cannot be valid because it is not historically factual.

4. Crews, "On the Importance of Political Theology in the Writings of Thomas Hobbes."

5. Pabst, in *Adam Smith as Theologian*, 110–11.

to rule over nature and make her captive and totally subservient to our will is deeply embedded in the modern outlook on knowledge and power, as Carolyn Merchant has well described.[6] Our elite global moneyed class— whom Susan George calls the Davos class[7]—also live as Olympian gods, apart from and over mere mortals, thanks to their financial dominance of the tiny globe.

Knowledge that is merely pragmatic is blind to meaning and value not of its own making, and is thus blind to the wonder of being and the transcendence that graces the cosmos in everything. This is dangerous knowledge because it has no reverence, no moral limits, no commitment to a harmonious difference and an ontology of goodness and love. Fear and hubris, producing both control and destruction, are readily the signatures of this knowledge.

To see knowledge grounded within being is to awaken to the full texture of our actual existence. This perspective requires the integration of knowledge with wisdom such that true knowledge—as full an understanding of the nature and meaning of the real as we can grasp—stands in front of its amoral, non-transcendently referenced shadow, that is "factual" and instrumental knowledge. As things now are, the shadow is blotting out the reality that casts the shadow.

Visioning "Good Faith" and "Right Belief" in a Meaningful Ontology as the Premise of Any Movement toward True Knowledge

It is not only the case that facts are delineated out from meanings by modern knowledge, but modern knowledge often sees itself as separated out from belief and from any need to have a commitment of good faith in any claim to true knowledge. Modern Technological Man seems to assume that the notion of proof, or at least of instrumental effectiveness, has made any sort of receptive trust obsolete in knowledge. However, the things that can be known cannot be "proven" in the categories of modern knowledge. Good faith is necessary for truth. Truth is necessary for a meaningful experience of actual reality.

Let me try to get to this via a very brief peek at Descartes's cogito.[8]

---

6. Merchant, *The Death of Nature.*

7. George, *Shadow Sovereigns*, 3–4.

8. Descartes foundation of epistemic certainty is often expressed as "cogito ergo sum"

Something Descartes grasps deeply—which he learns from Sextus Empiricus—is that no positive conception of knowledge can arise from skepticism. Knowledge and skepticism are not *actually* compatible. Empiricus, rejecting induction, replaces knowledge with habit and seeks to replace truth with *ataraxia* (peace of mind produced by the suspension of judgment and an accepting indifference to all feeling). Hume continues with Empiricus' approach, but Descartes wants knowledge and truth. Without going into it in detail, Descartes is in this regard aligned with Plato. Plato thinks that those who play rhetorical and instrumental games with reasoning and knowledge because of the genuine impossibilities of both empirical proof and linguistically expressed argumentative proof show bad faith to both reason and knowledge, and thus fail to take the actuality of our metaxological experience of existence seriously.[9]

Descartes grasps that skepticism must be overcome in order to have knowledge. However, where Descartes falters—as Kierkegaard points out—is in thinking that doubt leads you, step by step, to certainty, and that the thinking "I" is a social and spiritual atom.[10] Firstly, there is trust involved in every step of doubt, for one must trust the truth-revealing powers of the reasoning and observing process itself. Secondly, the concluding truth of any passage of rational "skeptical" steps is a decisive departure from the chain of doubt—an existential leap—and not an inevitable rational necessity. Thirdly, our understanding of the sociology of knowledge now makes it clear that human communities, language, indeed nothing short of the rich life-world in which any living human being knows, form the deep webs of mutuality, imagination, value, meaning, transcendence, and trust out of which a human knowledge of reality arises.

Faith is also basic to commerce. Market confidence (*con fide*; literally, with faith) is what actually makes the mundane financial transactions serving our day-to-day physical necessities possible. Our complex societies with their astonishing divisions of labor, staggering systems of transportation and supply, and enormous urban infrastructures simply would not operate if people did not trust the good will and mutual obligations that we

---

("I think therefore I am"). This, Descartes thought, was a certain truth that one could not rationally doubt.

9. Plato, *The Sophist.*

10. See Kierkegaard, *Philosophical Fragments*, on Kierkegaard's critique of methodological doubt. See Kierkegaard, *Sickness Unto Death*, on Kierkegaard's conception of the impossibility of the atomic "I."

collectively invest in each other via the social constructions of money and the rule of law.

Faith is a central enabling feature of the most materially concerned aspects of our lives (remunerated work and purchasing), and is often indirectly religious as we fetishize and worship the creations of our own imagination (financial wealth). Money would not work if people did not trust each other and were not willing to "play" a collective belief game with each other concerning the "value" of money. Further, faith is a centrally enabling feature of any community of knowers. Yet somehow enlightened and technologically powerful Man likes to think that we have dispensed with all substantive commitments we cannot objectively or "purely" rationally demonstrate, and we have left the irrational age of superstition and religion behind us.

Visioning faith as integral with knowledge and being is to recognize the metaxological nature of our being in the world. Here, knowledge is never either of pure transcendence (rationalism/idealism) or of pure immanence (empiricism/pragmatism), but is always an existential venture of good faith. This venture is always situated within a partial grasp of essential truths embedded in contingent and temporal contexts. The methodology of doubt and certain proof are not, finally, suitable to the texture of reality as we experience it.

6

ONTOPIA

The now dominant life-world sense of forgotten being, pragmatic knowing, and subjective believing is, in most regards, dangerously out of touch with the human and meaningful realities of our actual existence. We have lost an ontological consciousness in Western culture, and this loss has radically shaped our modern conception of what knowledge and belief are. We now have a conception of knowledge that is reductively quantitative, mathematical, and instrumental such that quality and transcendence are excluded from the realm of knowledge and technology. We now have a conception of belief that is so radically subjectivized and discrete from objective knowledge that we (ironically) believe that no existential commitment of good will toward the meaning and value of the cosmos that stands over us is required from us. This makes existentially committed belief into a discretely private matter that has no relevance to knowledge (and scholarship) or power or community life. This forgetting of being makes value and meaning as we experience it in our actual existence strangely outside of what it is possible to speak of with any knowledge or publicly concerned belief commitment. This leaves power in the hands of amoral pragmatists who have learnt how to be functionally blind to the value and meaning in which our actual existence is embedded. Thus, we have built a life-world of instrumental efficiency that is blind to value and meaning. The "necessity" of amoral instrumental power, driven to meaningless aims—survival, mere competitive victory, mere sensate pleasure, fearful and destructive self-preservation—is the only conception of "realism" known to our life world. We cannot reasonably control these meaningless "necessities" to avoid war, environmental disaster, or to impose moral and the political constraints on transnational corporations. We cannot control dangerous financial inventiveness, not simply because it is hard to put limits on wealth and power, but because the very ideas of moral truth and intrinsically valuable purposes are now outside our understanding of knowledge and power. If we were to insert a meaningful conception of being back into Western culture, it would also imply a radical life-world re-configuration.

According to the Czech philosopher Michael Hauser, politics as we now practice it in the Liberal Democratic West is dying.[1] Financialization has subverted the substantive meaning of popular sovereignty at the same time as the formal processes of liberal democracy have remained in place. As I read it, this is a natural consequence of an inadequate ontology, an instrumental value-free understanding of knowledge and a subjectivised conception of what belief and existential commitment actually are.

What our political, military, and economic theoreticians call "realism" is at the core of our life-world sickness. For a "realist" (ironically) believes that power is only about power. Here power is not an activated potentiality to achieve some inherently valuable purpose, rather power is merely the ability to consolidate and expand instrumental power. It is assumed that self-interest is the only real motive of rational human action, and that the only real definitions of self-interest are the satisfaction of material needs, the capacity to fulfill sensual desires, and a lack of inhibition regarding the pursuit of one's personal "value" preferences. That is, the "realism" assumed here is bereft of any ontological bearings. The wonder of being, the sense that existence is a gift, that the cosmos is alive with a Logos that we did not generate—that generates us!—that value and meaning are realities, that the harmony of beings is governed by timeless being, which itself is gifted to the cosmos by the ground of being (God); none of this penetrates the mind and aims of the modern realist. As such, politics is *only* the art of gaining and keeping political power (by whatever means work) and it is assumed that voters *only* have pragmatic materialistic goals, and that "values" are plastic marketing tools—political brands—that are thin veneers hiding the "real" drivers of the polity, fear, and greed. In short, our politics has become sub-human and is no longer responsive to actual human realities.

---

1. Hauser, "The Twilight of Liberal Democracy."

Ironically, we now live in a highly abstract and instrumentally governed utopia. Utopia, in Greek, means "no place" because *ou* (*ouk*) means "not" and *topos* means "place." Thomas More called his imaginative vision of a society without money or greed "utopia" to let the reader know this was an imagined place, not a real place. That it was also a *eu* (well, fortunate) *topos* (place) is significant in More's great classic, but the actual name means "no place." What we badly need now is the ability to somehow (though always in part) see the *ontos* (real) *topos* (place) in which we actually have our life and being. For we are enchanted by the fictive, the virtual, the possible, the "transcendence" of space and time, the projective *un*reality of the modern consumer life-world, which threatens to entirely replaced actual reality in our way of thinking about knowledge and power. What we need is some hunger to at least partially know the ontopia of our actual human existences.

I appreciate that in coining the word "ontopia" I am playing a rather complex terminological game. To Plato *ontos onta*—real beings—do not exist in space and time because they do not have a beginning or end and are always what they are (they do not become and unbecome as every spatio-temporal existing being does). And yet, the metaxological realm of our actual existence—our existential *topos*—is "located" *between* changeless and essential eternal being and spatio-temporal contingent flux. Thus, existence is a realm where concrete particular reality is always related to eternal meaning, value, and ideas, but where existence can never be reduced to the merely material and contingent, and where the material and contingent can never be speculatively overcome in such a way that we have an immediate and full grasp of pure being. So the reality of our actual existence is neither fully material and pragmatic, nor purely intellective and spiritual; the actual is always *both* material and spiritual. Hence it is the appreciation of the metaxological texture of existential actuality that I wish to appeal to by using the term "ontopia," in direct contrast with the abstract reductivism of the merely materialist and instrumentalist "utopia" of power and knowledge within the modern consumerist life-world. Ontopia is a "place" where we have recovered a viable vision of being, knowing, and believing. This vision is alive to the wonder, meaning, value, and doxological joy of our actual existential experience of reality.

We can only become articulately aware of the place where we actually are by re-integrating being, knowing, and believing in our way of seeing the world. We need to return to the immediate vision of wonder and meaning of the child. That is, we need a converted mind. The New Testament word that is usually translated (badly) as "repentance" is the word *metanoia*. This word means, literally, "after mind," implying a change of mind from a before way of thinking/seeing/acting to an after way of thinking/seeing/acting. If we can see that the modern disintegrative life-form way of forgotten being, instrumental knowing, and subjective believing does not align with the actual realities of human existence, then we are going to be open to *metanoia*. Then, perhaps, we might find, or be found by, a new way of being alive in the world, the real world, the world we actually exist in.

BIBLIOGRAPHY

Aquinas, Thomas. *Quaestiones Disputatae de Veritate Q. 1—9*. Translated by Robert W. Mulligan. Chicago: Regnergy, 1952.

Arendt, Hannah. *Eichmann in Jerusalem: A Report on the Banality of Evil*. New York: Penguin Classics, 1977.

Aristotle. *Complete Works*. Edited by Jonathan Barnes. Princeton: Princeton University Press, 1984.

Asad, Talal. *Formations of the Secular: Christianity, Islam, Modernity*. Stanford: Stanford University Press, 2003.

Augustine. *Against the Academicians, The Teacher*. Translated by Peter King. Indianapolis: Hackett, 1995.

Blondel, Maurice. *Action: Essay on a Critique of Life and a Science of Practice*. South Bend, IN: University of Notre Dame Press, 1984

Boyce, James. *1835: The Founding of Melbourne and the Conquest of Australia*. Melbourne: Black Inc., 2012.

———. *Born Bad: Original Sin and the Making of the Western World*. Melbourne: Black Inc., 2014.

Brown, Lesley. "The Verb 'to be' in Greek Philosophy: Some Remarks." In *Language*, edited by Stephen Everson, 212–37. Companions to Ancient Thought. Cambridge: Cambridge University Press, 1994.

Brunn, Emile Zum. *St. Augustine: Being and Nothingness*. New York: Paragon, 1988.

Buber, Martin. *I and Thou*. Edinburgh: T. & T. Clark, 1958.

Cannane, Steve, et al. "'Matter of Death and Life': Espionage in East Timor and Australia's Diplomatic Bungle." ABC Lateline, 26 Nov 2015. http://www.abc.net.au/news/2015-11-25/east-timor-greater-sunrise-spy-scandal/6969830.

Cobbing, Madeline. "Toxic Tech: Not in Our Backyard," Greenpeace International, 2008. http://www.greenpeace.org/international/Global/international/planet-2/report/2008/2/not-in-our-backyard.pdf.

Crews, Chris. "On the Importance of Political Theology in the Writings of Thomas Hobbes." 2009. file:///C:/Users/User%20PC/Downloads/Tracing_the_Theological_On_the_Importanc%20(1).pdf.

Das, Satyajit. *Extreme Money: The Masters of the Universe and the Cult of Risk*. Upper Saddle River, NJ: FT Press, 2011.

———. *Traders, Guns and Money: Knowns and Unknowns in the Dazzling World of Derivatives*. Upper Saddle River, NJ: FT Press, 2006.

Davies, Paul. *The Mind of God: Science and the Search for Ultimate Meaning*. London: Penguin, 1993.

Desmond, William. *The Intimate Strangeness of Being*. Washington, DC: Catholic University of America Press, 2012.

Dueweke, Robert F. "The Augustinian Theme of Harmony." PhD diss., Saint Paul University, Ottawa, Canada, 2004. http://www.tepeyacinstitute.com/uploads/6/9/1/4/6914821/final_thesis_for_publication.pdf.

Ferguson, Charles. *Inside Job: The Financiers Who Pulled Off the Heist of the Century*. London: Oneworld, 2012.

George, Susan. *Shadow Sovereigns: How Global Corporations are Seizing Power*. Oxford: Polity, 2015.

Gerson, Lloyd P. *Aristotle and Other Platonists*. Ithaca, NY: Cornell University Press, 2005.

Hamann, Johann Georg. "Metacritique on the Purism of Reason." In *Hamann: Writings on Philosophy and Language*, edited by Kenneth Haynes, 205–18. Cambridge: Cambridge University Press, 2007.

Hart, David Bentley. *The Experience of God: Being, Consciousness, Bliss*. New Haven: Yale University Press, 2013.

Hauser, Michael. "The Twilight of Liberal Democracy: A Symptomatic Reading of Depoliticization." *Décalages* 1.3 (2014). http://scholar.oxy.edu/decalages/vol1/iss3/4.

Hayek, Friedrich A. *The Road to Serfdom*. Chicago: University of Chicago Press, 1944.

Hil, Richard. *Whackademia: An Insider's Account of the Troubled University*. Sydney: NewSouth, 2012.

Kierkegaard, Søren. *Concluding Unscientific Postscript to Philosophical Fragments*. Edited and translated by Howard and Edna Hong. Princeton: Princeton University Press, 1992.

———. *Philosophical Fragments*. Edited and translated by Howard and Edna Hong. Princeton: Princeton University Press, 1985.

———. *The Sickness Unto Death*. Edited and translated by Howard and Edna Hong. Princeton: Princeton University Press, 1980.

Klein, Naomi. *The Shock Doctrine: The Rise of Disaster Capitalism*. London: Penguin, 2008.

Kuhn, Thomas S. *The Structure of Scientific Revolutions*. Chicago: University of Chicago Press, 1962.

Lewis, Michael. *The Big Short: Inside the Doomsday Machine*. New York: Norton, 2010.

Marx, Karl. *Introduction to a Contribution to the Critique of Hegel's Philosophy of Right*. First published in *Deutsch-Französische Jahrbücher*, Paris, 1844. https://www.marxists.org/archive/marx/works/1843/critique-hpr/intro.htm.

Merchant, Carolyn. *The Death of Nature: Women, Ecology, and the Scientific Revolution*. New York: HarperOne, 1989.

Milbank, John. *Theology and Social Theory*. 2nd ed. Oxford: Blackwell, 2006.

Nagel, Thomas. *Mind and Cosmos: Why the Materialist Neo-Darwinian Conception of Nature Is Almost Certainly False*. Oxford: Oxford University Press, 2012.

Niccol, Andrew, producer and director. *Lord of War*. Distributed by Lionsgate Films, USA, 2005.

Pabst, Adrian. "From Civil to Political Economy: Adam Smith's Theological Debt." In *Adam Smith as Theologian*, edited by Paul Oslington, 106–24. London: Routledge, 2011.

Plato. *Complete Works*. Edited by John M. Cooper. Indianapolis: Hackett, 1997.

Ronson, Jon. *The Psychopathy Test*. London: Picador, 2011.

Schindler, David C. "The Community of the One and the Many: Heraclitus on Reason." *Inquiry* 46.4 (2003) 413–48.

Schmitt, Charles B. *Aristotle and the Renaissance*. Cambridge: Harvard University Press, 1983.

Shaxson, Nicholas. *Treasure Islands: Tax Havens and the Men Who Stole the World*. London: Vintage, 2012.

Singer, Peter L. *Wired for War: The Robotics Revolution and Conflict in the 21st Century*. New York: Penguin, 2009.

Taibbi, Matt. *Griftopia: Bubble Machines, Vampire Squids, and the Long Con That Is Breaking America*. New York: Spiegel & Grau, 2010.

Taylor, Charles. *A Secular Age*. Cambridge: Belknap, Harvard University Press, 2007.

Varoufakis, Yanis. *And the Weak Suffer What They Must? Europe, Austerity, and the Threat to Global Security*. New York: Nation, 2016.

———. *The Global Minotaur: America, Europe, and the Future of the Global Economy*. London: Zed, 2011.

Milton Keynes UK
Ingram Content Group UK Ltd.
UKHW040628120924
1607UKWH00035B/313